R & R

Restoration and Redemption

A Personal Reflection of the 23rd Psalm

Bryn K Tucker

ISBN 979-8-9945419-0-6

Printed in USA by Bryn Tucker

References:

Young, Sarah. *Jesus Calling: devotions for every day of the year*. Liturgical, 2008. Print.

Table of Contents

Gratitude

To my dearest Scott, thank you for believing in me when I did not believe in myself. Thank you for calling out what you saw in me, that which I had yet to see for myself. Even in our darkest hours, you saw a light deep within. You are my rock, my lover, my favorite and I adore you. Love, J.J.

To my precious children, thank you for asking the hard questions, listening to my endless answers and revelations, allowing me to feel and dive deeper into what the Lord was showing me. You never tired of my epiphanies. Thank you. Thank you for reminding me when I was off track, Miss Lauren, and challenging me, praying for me, to finish what the Lord had started so long ago.

To my precious Oma, my kindred soul sister, my dear grandmother and writing buddy. You have inspired me in more ways than I will ever have the words to share. Thank you for never letting up on me and pushing me to get this book into the world. Thank you for being entirely you. You have certainly left me, and this world, better than you found it.

This book would not be if it were not for the love and support, encouragement, and direction of so many friends and family, far too many to name. The lives touched by this book are to your credit. You believed in me. You empowered me to do the work set out for me. Thank you.

Thank You, Father, for placing this call on my life, to write Your words and tell them that You did it. You are my Shepherd and my King. To You alone be the glory. Thank You for allowing me to be a pen in Your hand, writing this book as my purest act of worship to You.
I love You so!
Bryn

Forward

I believe God foreshadows events in our life and then, when the other crushing events come, reminds us of how we got through them before. Perhaps my grandmother had taught me the 23 psalm just by reading or saying it to me often when I was little. However it happened, I knew those words. Just when I needed them.

When I first read Bryn Tucker's book about the 23rd Psalm, I thought: "I know-I know all about this. I've taught it before in Sunday School and quoted it to hurting persons." But, I didn't. I don't. Because, each time you are in deep need of a certain promise in scripture, you may be positive—God will OFFER a UNIQUE contract with you, just you alone, and teach you new understandings through its familiar words.

I had the joy of babysitting Bryn many times. Also, She and another grandchild spent two weeks for five years, each summer with us so they could attend a Lab School for teachers in the 8 states and 17 Annual Conferences of the United Methodist Church at Mount

Sequoyah. Her joy in life, her imaginative play and her soft throaty chuckle brought me peace: I nicknamed her: "My Little Dove". Her childish faith: sparked a renewal of my own.

In her teen through early twenties, she survived an unexpected pregnancy and several years of difficult marriage. But, during troubled years, she stayed close to God and God strengthened her to work her own way through college cum laude. She worked at house cleaning, as a nanny and a business person. The church she attended provided a close group of young women who helped each other and were close in their faiths. Her mother was always there for her. From all of that, her own family evolved into a close binding relationship. Bryn became a teacher, ministry leader, as well as writing a children's book of gratitude.

In this book, you will feel her tender, honest, caring counsel. She can be your mother, sister, best friend, grandmother or teacher, as she guides you through your interaction with her written words and an experience with Christ. If you have never found the inner witness, this may be the book she has dedicated to you. Or, like for me, it may call you to a renewal of vows to follow Christ and love his people.

Bryn is God's catalyst. She does not insist on her own way but is a conduit for Jesus's parable of the "One" who cares, guards, enfolds each of us in His protective love.

- Constance Norton Waddell-Bryn's Oma,
Soul Sister and Writing Buddy
Forward written at age 96.

Preface

Like many of you, the only time I ever heard the 23rd Psalm was at a funeral or memorial service. Psalm 23 was forever tied to death, until the Lord began to reveal a new perspective on King David's words. Piece by piece, year upon year, I felt the Lord giving me new words and fresh revelation of what the twenty-third Psalm really meant. The words came to life on the well-worn pages of my Bible and in the ripening of my heart.

Something you should know, I am a Bible eater. By that I mean, I like to write all over my Bible and make notes and thoughts all throughout as I read. I always tell my children that I like to digest my Bible, not just read it.

One day I got to a point where I had run out of room to write notes around the 23rd Psalm and it struck me that I needed to share all of these little revelations and aha moments with others. Maybe others thought like I did, that Psalm 23 was a funeral passage. Maybe others needed the unique hope that David offers through his words. So, I set out to get my notes and thoughts and revelations out of my Bible and onto paper.

I believe that Lord is inviting you on a journey with me to a place, down by a still river, at a banquet set just for you, a place for a little R & R. A place that will tell the story of King David, of me and of course you. A place that will tell of your great restoration and redemption.

Welcome, friend, to your R&R!

Introduction

When the Lord put this book on my heart, and I set out to write it, I just knew it would be a women's ministry Bible study. I made the cover out of a beautiful picture my daughter, Lauren had taken. I even began writing the book. Then, I had dinner with my friend.

She and I caught up on all thing's wife and mommy and the conversations moved to our personal walks. When it was my turn, I could not wait to show her the cover of the book that Lauren and I had poured our hearts into. As I showed her my newborn idea, I gushed all of the details I just knew God wanted me to set my book around. She said something that hit me hard, "It looks like a devotional." "Well, that is all good and well, but He gave me a book to write", I thought to myself, "not a daily devotional." My word, I was so prideful.

For months, I stewed over the innocent comment and tried to write the study I knew I was supposed to write. But I was wrong. My sweet friend knew something I did not, I had a daily devotional to write.

The Lord has humbled me and shown me that this R&R is all about a daily walk, not just six-week study.

Life is lived one day at a time, not in preplanned chunks. It's not neat or tidy. Its messy and at times, quite uncomfortable.

I believe in morning devotions. Just like in the principal of tithing, if you give your ten percent after your bills are paid and the groceries have been bought, dinners eaten out, you will not have ten percent leftover to give. If you wait till the end of the day, you may find you are too tired, too worn out, to process the Word of God.

Now, as a sister who has walked the road of legalism ahead of you, please hear me say, our Heavenly Father wants to be with you all day long. He does not require any acts from you to love you perfectly. In fact, you could put this book down right now, and He would love you just the same. If you are in a season where the babies are up before the rooster crows and the sun's first light shines, and you haven't the time to shower every day, enjoy this book during a nap time or in those overnight feeding times when the baby thinks that midnight is the new noon and won't go back to sleep. When the season comes, and it will, that you have the luxury of waking up before the children, try starting your day with the Lord.

Since starting the R & R devotional, a year ago, I have struggled to see how I was to write it and finish it. Another amazing friend, spoke over my thirty-seventh birthday, saying that I would receive "fresh revelation" and that I would finish my book in this year. No kidding, a year after starting this process, the Lord revealed to me that the book study must be written, as well as the devotional. It is just like me to jump right up the minute I hear one thing from the Lord. Turns out it was a comma, not a period at the end of what He said. So here I am, writing a book again, humbled, and transparent, tired, and worn out from trying to do things my own way with only half of what I needed to know.

My friend was onto something. I needed to get out of my own preconceived way, to let the Lord reveal His plans. I pray that you will do the same. We often pick up a book study and think it is something, but the truth is, this book will be what you put into it and what you plead with God to reveal to you out of it.

Let us go to the Father now and ask Him for His blessing.

Father,

I give this book back to You. May it be Your words, written for You, my audience of one. Please forgive my hastiness, my presumptions, my pride. I need Your help as I dive in, to excavate into the very depths of Your word. Let it be a fresh revelation. I cannot write this book without Your words. I long to be the pen in Your hands. Please be the ink that flows through, writing on the pages of all of our hearts.

I love You so,

Bryn

The Lord is my shepherd;
I shall not want.
Psalms 23:1

Not a Stranger

For you formed my inward parts; you knitted me together in my mother's womb. I praise you, for I am fearfully and wonderfully made. Wonderful are your works; my soul knows it very well. Psalm 139:13-14

My mother loves to knit. When I say love, I mean love. She's not quite the lady who takes her knitting to the opera, but she does enjoy blessing her loved ones with her yarn creations. One of my favorite gifts she has given me is the lush, warm, ivory colored blanket my children all love to steal and claim as their own.

Long before I knew she decided to make this gift for me, she had to choose the right color yarn to use. Then, she had to decide the texture she wanted it to have, how heavy or light it would be. She had to decide what pattern she would employ to make her creation. Once she finalized her plan, she set off to bless me with a wonderful blanket. One that would warm my body and spirit for years to come.

Each time the pattern would get off, or a stitch was messed up, she unraveled it and began again. She didn't allow errors to mess up her craft. I have seen her take apart an entire piece, because one stitch threw off her entire project. She is not a perfectionist by any measure, but this work of heart is important to her. Each detail is as important as the one before it.

When the day finally came, and my birthday arrived, she proudly presented her masterpiece. It was and still is perfectly made. In fact, I am covered with it right now as I write to you.

Our Heavenly Father has done the same with each one of us. He has chosen every fabric and strand in which to create us. He knows every detail that went into our creation. He made no mistakes in making you. You are no stranger to Him. He is our Shepherd. He is not only our guide, but the one who brought us into existence. Isaiah 43:7 says:

"everyone who is called by my name, whom I created for my glory, whom I formed and made."

The creator of the Universe made you, for His glory. Another translation reads for His pleasure. Our great

Shepherd took immeasurable care and attention to detail and created us, for Himself and for His glory and His pleasure. At any given point, He could have completely unraveled you, and created someone entirely different, but He did not. You were no mistake. He did not mess anything up in your creation. You, at your intentionally created core, are exactly who He fashioned you to be. And He made you complete, lacking in nothing but your need for more of Him. He made you enough. Enough today, and enough tomorrow.

Before we move on, I think it is critical to stop and acknowledge our creation, our making in the Potter's hands. Society would love for us to believe that we are made wrong; that we are a mistake. Some of us believe that maybe we were made right, but we have made so many mistakes that we have undone all the good that was originally done in us. The fabric of our lives is fearfully and wonderfully made, not fearfully or pitifully made. Do you know that you were made in His image? Is He flawed? Depending on the life you have known to this point, your view of our Creator just might be less than perfect, thus leading to the idea that you, too, might be imperfectly made, especially if made in His image.

But can I speak into your life for a moment? I believe that you are perfectly made and perfectly loved by a perfect Creator God. I believe the world is trying to rob you, rob me, rob everything and everyone as we know, from the peace that comes from knowing we were made in His image, perfect and complete. Pastor Michael Todd reminds us that our perfectly made includes our whole selves. It includes the things that make me quirky, weird, off-putting, obnoxiously, encouragingly, optimistic. All of it. The world needs all of me, and all of you. So, we have got to put to the side this phony bologna notion that our flaws make us less of who He made us to be! I pray today, right this moment, that you begin to know how very intentionally and perfectly you were made, in His image. I pray that today, you get a glimpse of the incredible, irreplaceable role you, you in all your imperfectly perfect self, play in this time you have been given to walk this earth.

I am talking to me.

Thank you, Father, for taking such incredible care to make me. Thank you for choosing each piece of me. Thank you for making me to be so specifically me, unlike everyone else, so that I can do what you have called me alone to do! Please help me to remember that I am your wonderfully made creation, made in Your image alone.

Amen

My Source

Jesus said to her, "Everyone who drinks of this water will be thirsty again, but whoever drinks of the water that I will give him will never be thirsty again. The water that I will give him will become in him a spring of water welling up to eternal life." John 4:13-14

Most every morning I wake up to a little blue or green flashing light. By this I know there are notifications that someone has commented on a post, or messaged me, on social media, sent an email or a text. My need for instant gratification wants to check and see exactly why I have a light flashing on my phone. However, I know that if I check to find out the source of the lights flashing, I could spend anywhere from one to ten minutes, or, who am I kidding, way more of my morning scrolling mindlessly through pictures and statuses. I can kill time like it's my part time job, especially from the comfort of my warm bed and snuggly pajamas! Ever had something you needed to do, but were dragging your feet by scrolling through your newsfeed? Me too! As a teacher, I cannot tell you how many batteries I have drained in attempts to avoid grading a stack of papers.

As a mom of five amazing children, quality quiet time is a rare commodity and often in short supply. If I spend those valuable minutes in my time budget, mindlessly scrolling, I lose the opportunity to intentionally seek God's face. I only have so much time before all of the little faces want to be in my momma face and there is no more time for seeking God's face.

When I go first to the wrong "well" to be nourished, like the woman Christ met that day, I always come back from it thirstier than when I arrived. It will only satisfy my needs for a moment. I will have to return to it constantly for validation, approval, and "spiritual nourishment". Each ding, alert, or flashing light, calls me back to its emptiness.

The Psalmist knew where the "right" well was to drink from. He knew Who his eternal source was. He said, *"The Lord is my shepherd, I shall not want."* Why did he not want? Because all of his needs were fully met in the Lord. See, he did not need to go to others for validation in who he was. He need not go to a mystic for spiritual direction. The Psalmist knew who his shepherd was and that his needs were perfectly met in Him.

In the New Testament, Jesus finds Himself at a well in the middle of the day. This is the hottest time of the day. Texans, I want you to think noon in late August. You would not be caught dead outside at this time, or you might find yourself feeling like your feet are melting off as you are walking on the surface of the sun. This time of day is not when the women would have gathered at the well to get water. They would have been there much earlier in the day, not only to avoid the heat, but to have time to socialize and fellowship. This was exactly why the Samaritan woman went at noon. She was hiding her lifestyle, her questionable choices, from their heated, glaring judgement, much hotter than the noon day sun. Truth be told, she was hiding from herself.

Jesus knew exactly who the Samarian woman was. He knew when He met at the well that she had had many husbands. Instead of condemning her, He let her know that He knew her and loved her completely.

Can you imagine for one moment how she felt? This strange man walks up to you, knows all of your dirty laundry, knows why you are where you are, when you are there, and does not for a moment judge you for any of it. He doesn't want anything from you, or to be yet another lover or husband. He just selflessly loves you.

Can I tell you something? Please, lean in close, I really want you to hear me whisper this into your thirsty soul. He loves you.

He does. And He loves me too. Right here in the midst of it all, He loves me, and He loves you.

He revealed His identity to her and that He alone could provide the eternal source she so longed for. When we seek to find our source in anything other than Christ, we too, are taking on more "husbands." These pseudo-sources are the wrong well, and they leave us depleted and spiritually dehydrated. He alone, can deeply satisfy our parched souls. We do not come back to Him to be refilled, reloved, reapproved. We come back to Him because we just love Him, too.

For many years, well before social media tightened its grip around our lives, I worshiped my husband. I did not know that was what I was doing. Every mood he had, dictated my own. If he found me attractive, I felt pretty. If he was angry with me, I wracked my brain for what I could have done to lost favor and approval in his sight. I lived for what he thought of me. I often found myself hopeless, entertaining the idea of suicide. With no clear rules to follow, no underserved grace, no unconditional love, I could not please my husband, my little g god, completely. And this wrecked me. It consumed me until I realized what I was doing.

I was exiting the highway one afternoon when it hit me. I was worshiping my husband, a role he was never created to carry, the role of being my God. This whole vicious cycle nearly destroyed our marriage. It was too much pressure for him to shoulder the entire weight of my self-worth and identity. He was my wrong well and expecting him to be my source left us both parched and desperate. This led me to a place of asking God for forgiveness, for having another idol before Him.

This continued to be a struggle, off and on, for many years following. Sometimes healing and change came instantly, and sometimes over a longer period of time. Me being the stubborn person that I am, my path has taken me much longer, to finally get it through my thick skull. Some days it is easy. Some days I can see it for what it is and what I am doing, and other days, I cannot even tell that I have arrived at the wrong well, yet again. Just this afternoon, I found myself at the crossroads. He was irritated with me, and I had a choice: worship his approval of me or be certain of who I am in Christ. I chose the latter. I went to my Heavenly Father for my approval and it turns out, I am still secure in Him.

Are there idols that you have erected that have come to mind as you have been reading? Have you ever found yourself, like the woman at the well, avoiding being in fellowship with others because you know that they know you too well? Have you ever cowered and hidden yourself from the loving truth of a godly friend?

Let's go a little deeper, can we? Who or what is your source? Take a moment to reflect and pray, asking God to reveal these things to you. Not addressing these matters can leave you more parched than nourished, thirstier, and always lacking something more, your true Source. Hear me say to you, straight from the scars of my own heart, address these things, know them, really and truly know them. Putting a finger on it, rather than a Band-Aid on it, is key in getting help from the right well.

Please forgive me Father, for the many "wells" that I have run to, to be my source instead of you. If there are any unknown sources or idols in my life, please reveal them to me. You are my one and only. You alone satisfy my endless thirst with your endless love.

Amen

My Comfort

*For I, the Lord your God, hold your right hand; it is I
who say to you, "Fear not, I am the one who helps you."*
Isaiah 41:13

Every time I am out walking with my husband, he moves me to the inside of the road, between himself and the curb. If I am being honest, it kind of drives me crazy. For a long time, I wore my footstep counter on my right hand. For that thing to work, my arm has to be swinging and what happens when you hold hands and you are not eight, your arm does not swing. No swing, no steps recorded. I know, probably not a battle to pick, but this is why I would put myself on his right.

I think it is important to clarify that he does not prefer this spot as a position of power, but rather as a position of safekeeping and honor. He does this to deliberately put himself between me and the cars driving down the road. He chooses this position to be my source of safety. Our Heavenly Father takes the same position. I treasure that scripture even says that He holds our right hands.

"For I, the LORD *your God, hold your right hand; it is I who say to you, "Fear not, I am the one who helps you."*
Isaiah 41:13

Do you realize what that means? We are on His left side! This puts Himself between us and our world. He does not take this stance as a position of power, but rather He chooses this place for Him and for us to be our source of safety and aid, even honor.

He says to us in Isaiah 41:10, *"Fear not, I am the one who helps you."* Through His word, He tells us not to fear. This is not because the world isn't scary, because it so very much is. Nor is it because to fear is a sin, or because we think we can save ourselves, which, trust this try hard girl, you cannot. It is not because of any other reason than He alone is the one who truly helps us. What great comfort it brings to know that He is the one who helps us. When we view that which brings about fear, through the lens of the one who is our Helper, the fear tends to dissipate.

Remember, He sees the mountains ahead and knows the strength you will need to endure it. He also knows the path ahead you cannot see, even the path which He may choose to use to divert you around the looming mountain in the distance.

He is a gentleman. He is a Shepherd. He takes your right hand and places himself between you and the world. When he chose to endure the cross, he chose to place himself between you and the eternal death you were sentenced to. This sacrificial death was not an assertion of power and dominion. His death was an act of unconditional love. Your eternity is so precious that your sin-stained life was atoned for, once and for all, through this ultimate, loving act of mercy and grace.

I think it is important to stop and take a look at your beliefs on Christ's death. I am very serious. I think it is genuinely time to take an honest look deep within.

I grew up in the Methodist faith, and my friend grew up in the Baptist faith. She talked about things I had never really heard before. She talked about how I needed to be saved, a concept completely foreign to me as a child.

The very phrase made me squirm in my seat every time I heard it.

I was thirty-eight, leading a small group of college aged adults, when I had to share a question with them, asking how they felt about the concept of the Trinity. More specifically, if there a part of the concept of the Trinity that made them uncomfortable, or was more unfamiliar. There in that upstairs living room, I realized that though I had accepted Christ as my Lord and Savior, the whole concept of salvation was the most uncomfortable to me still.

I am a works-driven person. This goes hand in hand with my need to be a people person. Being driven to please and earn favor from others makes an unearnable salvation a brain bender. From time to time, I still struggle with the concept of undeserved, unearned grace and find myself working to pay God back, as if that were humanly possible! My feelings of unworthiness tend to drive that crazy train. I know that I am not worthy of the gift He has given me, and no amount of good work or good behavior will ever be good enough to say thank you for His death, for my eternity.

So, I go back to my original question to you, which I just realized I never actually asked, but totally intended to. What are your beliefs on Christ's death? What beliefs about His death were you taught growing up, if any? Do you feel like it is a power play or an act of love, or maybe even something completely different? I think it is imperative to delve into your beliefs about salvation. How do you relate to the idea of unearned salvation? Is this easy for you to receive, or does the need to work for it keep you from receiving it at all?

It is ok. Take a deep breath and look inside. Do not rush on to the next part just so that you can check a box. This book, this chapter, this section, *your salvation* is far too important to simply check a box. I know, I have read the books, led the studies, checked all of the boxes, and knew nothing of my own personal salvation.

Friend, please hear me. Slow down. It will all be there when you are done. Your eternal life is worth it. I wish with everything I have in me that I could tell you to close your eyes and let your heart listen as I pray over you. I wish you knew the tenderness I have for you in this season. How I wish I could look you in the eye and tell you that I know, and that it is ok to not be ok right now. Please take the time to be in this place with your Creator, sit at the edge of His eternal well and let Him pour Himself out, into your life. He longs for you, for this moment.

Father,

I thank you for your death on the cross, a death that has taken me so long to understand, even if still not completely. I lift up my sister who is sitting there, reading these words, tears streaming down her face. I pray that she would hear and know Your voice. Please forgive me for trying to repay you for this gift of salvation. Please help us all to fully grasp, to the best of our human ability, the depth of your love. Let us all feel your warmth today.

Amen

My Strength

*God is our refuge and strength, a very present help in
trouble. Psalm 46:1*

I am kind of a nerd about various parts of the Bible. One
of those little quirks of mine is my love of the teeny tiny
print, at the very bottom of the page, the footnotes.
These little bitty words, almost illegible, add so much
context to the scriptures above. They add in various
translations, or even word meanings. In the footnotes
of my Bible, there is a postscript note about the words
"very present." It says that in other translations, the
same verse reads "well proved." Take a moment, right
now, and reread those beautiful God-breathed lines of
the 46th Psalm with the alternative word choice,

*"God is our refuge and strength, a well proved help in
trouble."*

YES! Isn't it beautiful? He is a well proved help in
trouble, yours and mine and the lady bagging groceries,
yeah, her troubles, too! In the season I am in, those
words ring so brilliant and true. But it did not always

seem so true for me, in fact, in some of my darkest seasons, I felt that God had only proven Himself as being most absent in my pain.

Reality is, you do not have to be alive very long to see that you need help. From the very beginning, this living thing is quite complicated, and I am constantly putting myself in, or finding myself in, various situations that require assistance from someone else.

My marriage is no exception. Cue the harps and blurred intro and outro.

Scott and I married at eighteen, with only three months of friendship and "dating" under our belt. This made for quite a troubling start. Strike one! We both have older half siblings who lived with their mothers, so both of us were raised as predominantly only children. Another strike against us! We were young, immature, and so very selfish. Our marriage was a recipe for certain disaster. Many counted us out, long before we ever began. They had every reason under the sun to believe that we did not stand a snowball's chance in this whole marriage thing. And for the first ten years of our shell of a marriage, I believed what everyone else believed. Wholeheartedly, I believed we didn't stand a chance. I let everyone define my marriage, but God.

Do you remember what I said about needing help? Our marriage needed real help and a real savior. Left to our own tools, or the lack thereof, we were unable to change anything about ourselves or our marriage. All that was well proved about us, was that we had no idea what we were doing, even after ten, excruciatingly long years. Our marriage, our family, needed a well proved Shepherd to guide us and counsel us in the ways we should go.

In year eleven, we finally began to seek God regarding our marriage and family. He led us to a wonderful church family that would become a cornerstone for us to rebuild a family upon, starting with our marriage. He soon after led us to a marriage ministry that we would attend and later serve with for several years. Looking back, all of these events highlighted the presence of a present, well proved Savior and Shepherd in the troubles and trials, as well as the rebuilding of our lives. He was surely in it all, positioning Himself between us and the world.

This well proved, very present help became our strength, the strength of our marriage and family. This strength was something we did not have on our own. We were weak, worn out from never-ending battles, and just plain numb. We needed the strength that could only come from a well proved, very present Savior.

When we look back to verse one of the twenty-third Psalm, *"The Lord is my shepherd, I shall not want."* we see that our needs are met in Him alone. He is our source, our comfort, our strength.

What a Shepherd He has been. And just like any dumb sheep, we fought Him, much and often, certain we knew what we needed and when we needed it and doubted His sovereignty every time things did not go as planned.

Moses also asked God to reveal Himself to him, something so many of us has done. We want Him to show us His plan, His fingerprints, the holes in the palms of his hands. We want to see evidence that He is in this life with us, especially in those dark moments in the Valley of the Shadow of death.

Our gracious Father agrees to Moses' request saying:

"When my glory passes by, I will put you in a cleft in the rock and cover you with my hand until I have passed by. Then I will remove my hand and you." Exodus 33:22-23

I don't know about you, but I might be like, "God, I kind of meant that I wanted to, like, see you, see you, like your face, maybe? If that is ok? Totally ok if it is not. Up to you God." But God knew better. He knew that that for Moses to see His face would mean that Moses would die. So, He put Moses in a safe place, covered with His hand, and passed by. When He had safely made passage by, and only then, He removed His hand so that Moses could see His back.

Why am I bringing this up? How many times have you begged God to show you where He is, right in that deepest, darkest moment, and because He did not show you His face, you said that He must have left you behind? Because He didn't come sing Amazing Grace with you, because He did not come pluck you out of the situation you were in for YEARS, He must have abandoned you. How many times have you said those words? Oh, you haven't said them. You believed them. You internalized them. You taught them to your children by your actions of unbelief. Me too.

That dark moment, dark season, hidden in the cleft of a rock, shrouded by the very hand of God. Then, He removes His hand and for the first time, as the light begins to filter in, your eyes adjust just in time to see His back as He passes by. You see where He was all along. He never left you. You see for the first time how He was shielding you with His righteous right hand as He passed by. Could it be, you weren't ready to see Him yet?

I know I was not. I knew God, but I did not *know* Him at all. I would have been crushed by the weight of who He is, had He allowed me to see Him in those moments. The darkest of my seasons of life were so painFULL, yet, what do I know of how much He shielded me from? What was happening on the outside of the cleft He had placed me in? I thought what I was feeling, experiencing with all of my being was bad. What do I know of that which He never revealed to me on the other side of His hand? It wasn't until after the season that He allowed me to see His fingerprints all over everything! In reflection and remembering, I see He was always there, even in, especially in, my doubt.

Where are you right now? Are you in the cleft? Are your eyes shielded from His glory? Have you had the opportunity to reflect and see just how well proved and ever present He was? Does He seem absent and unaware? Does it feel like He has passed you by with no proof of His presence? Have you seen His back, in your looking back? Have you seen His well proved fingerprints all over your life as you looked back? He was there. He was always there.

Father,

I cannot thank you enough for your ever-present ways. Even when I could not see you, couldn't stick my doubting fingers in the holes of your hands, You were and are still, well proved. Please forgive me for ever believing, even for a moment that You would abandon me, for believing Your love for me could only carry me so far. Thank you for allowing me to see Your back and protecting me from Your face. Thank you for loving me even in my most unlovable seasons. I love you so!

Amen

Yield, Not Surrender

My mother tells of a time she was traveling with my grandmother. I think it important to note that my grandmother was the one at the wheel for this leg of the journey. At some point in their travels, they reached an on ramp for the highway, to which my grandmother entered and then came to a complete stop. My mom admittedly yelled, "It says 'YIELD', not SURRENDER!" Reluctantly, my grandma entered the highway, and they continued their journey, both a bit shaken up.

Don't we all do the same thing from time to time?

Let me tell you a little bit about my early story growing up. I grew up in a Christian home, daughter of a preacher and a teacher. I knew all the spiritual and earthly rules. Is it any wonder I fight legalism? I digress. I was also the baby of the family, which meant I got a front row seat to my older sister's life and all of her choices, good, bad or otherwise. Thus, I learned more of the special rules, the implied kind, the "learn from my mistakes" kind of rules. Armed with what *not* to do,

I set out on a life of trying to navigate what I *could* do. I quickly began making many of my own choices, running into many boundaries, and making my own mistakes.

At the age of fifteen I was already having sex. I knew the rule about not having sex till marriage, but I so desperately wanted to be loved and accepted and seen, that my body led the charge, not my moral compass, or anyone's preset rules. Halfway through my sixteenth year I hit an onramp to the biggest highway I had ever known, pregnancy. I had a choice. I could yield or surrender.

At first, I surrendered. I was scared out of my mind. What would I say to my family? To him? To my friends? What would the kids say when I returned to school in the Fall for my Junior year? What would the church say about me? To me? I was supposed to be the "good girl" in the church play. What about clothes, for me? For a baby? What about? What about? I was frozen. I was stopped in the middle of my life's new onramp, and I had no idea how to proceed.

My mom, again the great co-pilot, eased me onto the highway, helping me to yield to the new season of my life, not surrender. My mom shared the news of the pregnancy with my grandfather, who was also a preacher. On par for the mid-nineties, he sent us a letter in the mail. In it he said he would be down for a visit in three days. He said that he wanted to hug both of his girls. In his letter, he also shared a scripture from Numbers 6:24-26:

> The LORD bless you and keep you; the LORD make his
> face to shine upon you and be gracious to you;
> the LORD lift up his countenance upon you and give you
> peace.

Instead of judgement, instead of rejection and abandonment, my grandfather gave me grace. In three days' time, he came, and grace is exactly what he gave. The grace he gave on that visit, helped me to enter the fastest paced highway I had yet known. Though we were all a bit shaken up, we continued on our journey as a young, growing family.

We serve, love, and follow a mighty God, who instead of rejection and abandonment, showed up with undeserved, unmerited grace. Instead of allowing us to pay the penalty for our countless sins, paid them Himself, on the cross. In three days' time, He came for us, and it was grace He brought with Him. Even the thief on the cross, who called out to Christ at the very last moment of life, to remember him in Paradise, was adopted and accepted in an instant instead of complete rejection and abandonment. Matthew 18:12-13 puts it this way:

"What do you think? If a man has a hundred sheep, and one of them has gone astray, does he not leave the ninety-nine on the mountains and go in search of the one that went astray? And if he finds it, truly, I say to you, he rejoices over it more than over the ninety-nine that never went astray."

He, the Good Shepherd, is coming after you, looking for you. Do you know that He is not out to catch you? He is not trying to see if you are naughty or nice? He has left the ninety-nine because you are the one He notices, the one who needs Him most right now, and you know what, its ok. He longs to pick you up, to wrap you up in His loving arms of grace and return you to the safety of His fold. He makes His face to shine upon you, too.

You may be on the onramp to something scary, and it may feel like surrendering to your circumstances seems like the only logical and viable option, but it's not. Maybe this time, instead of surrendering to life, you yield to God. Yielding to Him may be scarier than the thing you are facing right now. It may be counterintuitive to believe, but His grace is more than enough. He is well-proved and ever present. His back will be seen by you. He has never left you. You are so important to Him, even in the midst of your onramp that He would leave watch to come find you. He would, while you were still a sinner, die your death, for you to have eternal life. You are that important. You were made for His glory, even if you feel like your life is not a reflection of that glory at this moment. You cannot change what He made in you. You just aren't that powerful. I'm not either.

Would you take a moment and pray with me? Would you let these words be yours, even if they do not make sense at this moment, this season of life? Would you allow yourself to believe, even for just a moment?

Father,

Thank you for coming for me. Thank you for noticing I had wandered off from your flock, following the distractions of the world and culture all around me. Thank you for your guidance, keeping me from stalling out on the onramps of my life. I thank you that when you arrived three days after the cross, you brought with you undeserved grace. Please never let me forget that grace, and that you are always here with me, well proved, ever present. Thank you that I am never alone, never abandoned. I am loved.

Amen

Sheep

Sheep are credited as being one of the most unintelligent animals to roam the earth. Though they are known for their lack of intelligence, they are also known for their obedience. They are faithful followers. These four-legged, wooly creatures know the sound of their shepherd's voice, and they are obedient to follow it. David knew the voice of his Shepherd, and he knew to follow it.

The twenty-third Psalm starts with King David acknowledging that God is his Shepherd. He realizes that he is not the king of his own world, but rather he is in submission to a higher power who will lead him.

Submission to authority scares many of us. The thought of giving control to another person, let alone an authority we cannot see, is frightening at best. Isn't it easier to read "I *shall not want.*" then "*The Lord is my Shepherd*"? A shepherd is in charge of his sheep. The sheep must be in submission to their leader.

Take a moment of reflection. What are your thoughts on submission? What has been taught, or better yet, what has been "caught" by observing the world around you? Maybe your view of submission is one that is positive. Maybe it is one that is negative. Does the very idea bring you great comfort, or does it make your skin crawl with total disgust? How did your parents relate to one another? It is critical that you understand what your beliefs of submission are so that you can identify the lens in which you view it, and fully grasp how it colors your life, even your views on faith and God's place as the shepherd of your life. If your views of submission are negative, the thought of submitting to Him might be the last thing you want to do. If your views are positive, it might bring you great relief to submit to God's place as Shepherd over your life. Either way, I pray you will do the hard work, ask the hard questions of yourself, and identify the ways in which you view God's place in your life.

I think it is important to stop and look at the words 'yield' and 'surrender.' I am a teacher by training and vocation. I love to dig into words, and I am sure you have noticed, I think it is imperative to stop every so often to dig deeper into the Word, and into our own selves.

According to Merriam-Webster, the word "yield" means to give way to or become succeeded by someone or something else. In contrast it states that the word "surrender" means to give up completely or agree to forgo especially in favor of another. Submission is a hot button word for my generation of women. The very thought makes many people cringe. Our current culture views submission as total surrender. They see submission as giving up ones' self to another and losing their own lives in the process. It is often seen as laying down one's thoughts, feelings, and opinions to become a voiceless, powerless doormat for another person. This couldn't be further from the truth.

Biblical submission to the Lord, our example for all of life's needs, is one of yielding. We are giving way to the

Lord. We are allowing Him to go before us. To lead us. Much like the sheep, we are allowing Him to shepherd us. Jesus told the disciples,

"My sheep hear my voice, I know them, they follow me."
John 10:27

He is talking about us. He knows us and our response is to simply follow Him. Knowing Him, truly knowing Him, makes it a joy for me to follow Him. I no longer feel that He is insufficient, or feel the need to lead Him, or leave Him behind me.

The uncomfortable truth is, He surrendered His life, completely, in favor of another. That "another", is you and me, and the life He gave, He gave completely, so that you and I could have an eternity with Him.

"Just as the Father knows me and I know the Father;
and I lay down my life for the sheep." John 10:15

He did not yield Himself for us. Read that again. He laid down His life, He surrendered His life for you, for me.

If you have not yielded your life to Christ, accepting Him as your Lord and Savior, there is no time like the present. Your Shepherd loves you so much that He would die on a tree and usher in grace three days later, to save your eternal life. Would you ask Him now, to forgive you of your sins, to lead your life, to shepherd you? He has surely waited for this glorious moment with you, with all of us. As author, Angie Smith states in her book *Mended*, "The nails didn't keep Jesus on the tree. Love did."

Father, thank You for allowing us to yield to You, our Shepherd, and then surrendering Your own life for ours. Help us to see the difference in our yielding to You, and Your surrender for us. May we see your choice of love, to stay on the cross for each of us, and give the ultimate act of thanks by accepting Your perfect gift.

Amen

Penguins

As a third-grade teacher, I loved teaching the children about Emperor penguins. These tiny, tuxedo donning birds strangely fascinate me. One of the reasons I am wowed by these animals is their ability to recognize specific voices. The Emperor penguin has a unique way of knowing it's mate's voice. They use this ability to stay in communication with each other, most importantly when one is returning from many months of hunting for sustenance. They call out to each other, and then listen for the reply of the other.

Jesus echoes the same is true for the followers of Christ when he shared the parable of the sheep and the shepherd with his disciples in John 10.

When he has brought out all his own, he goes before them, and the sheep follow him, for they know his voice.
(v. 4)
I am the good shepherd. I know my own and my own know me, (v. 14)
My sheep hear my voice, and I know them, and they follow me. (v. 27)

In these scriptures, Jesus points us back to the very first verse of the 23rd Psalm, that He is the Good Shepherd, and if we are followers, we know His voice and follow Him, and we shall never want. In His parable, He even illustrates the image that would point to His coming crucifixion. He talks about how the Good Shepherd would lay down his own life for his sheep. (v 11)

When I read the words, "I *lay down my life.*" (v15) I see Old Testament sacrifices. I see Christ foreshadowing the ultimate sacrifice, that He would lay himself down, the one spotless lamb, on a wooden alter, once and for all sin.

This is a powerful principal King David understood. He knew his Father's voice, called out to Him in desperation and then he listened eagerly for the reply from his Shepherd. Psalm 143:8 shows us a glimpse of King David's desire to hear his Shepherd's voice:

"Let me hear in the morning of your steadfast love, for in you I trust. Make me know the way I should go, for to you I lift up my soul." Psalm 143:8

We start by seeing that King David knows his heavenly Father's voice. Think of the gravity of that. A king's world is rarely silent, rather it is filled with the clamoring voices of multitudes of people, opinions, suggestions, declarations. The Lord's voice is a *"low whisper."* (1 Kings 19:12) If then, it is as faint as a low whisper, or written in other translations *"a still small voice"*, it would take incredible intentionality, even discernment, on David's part to hear from God. And he not only heard from his Shepherd, but he also recognized his Shepherd's voice.

David pleads with God to let him hear from Him in the morning. He is desperate and seeking an answer right away, all the while affirming that his trust is in God alone. He begs that God would show him the way to go. He is seeking counsel from his Maker. He is yielding to his Shepherd. He does all of this in total, intentional, and willful submission.

In this way, King David is much like the Emperor penguin. He sought to hear the voice and he heard it. But what makes him most like the penguins is that he responds to it. He goes toward God. He does not just hear from God, he pursues Him and advances. Imagine if the penguins heard their mate's voices and just stayed put. There is no point for this unique gift if all they do is hear each other. The same is true for our unique ability to hear the Lord. It is a pointless gift if we do nothing with it, and all we do is hear.

We must respond, like David, making our way, closer and closer to God, our Shepherd.

Unlike King David, is King Saul. Saul, in 1 Samuel 13, is commanded by Samuel to wait seven days to make an offering to God. Sounds easy enough, right? Just wait? But, put this into context. Saul was at war and his enemy's presence was imminent. His troops were getting restless and fearful of what they could physically see coming at them. On the seventh day, impatiently waiting for Samuel to return, and no

Samuel in sight, King Saul takes matters into his own insecure hands and offers the sacrifice to God.

At that moment, Samuel arrives and questions his actions. Saul tries to defend his actions. Samuel ultimately tells Saul that this very act has removed God's purpose for his life. Saul heard God's direction, His voice, through Samuel. And for seven days, he obeyed. And then, he let his senses lead the charge. He did not act on what God called him to do. He acted on what his troops said he should do. Even in an offering, a sacrifice to God, he acted out of fear, rather than faith and robbed himself of his God given destiny.

When God speaks, when we are intentional to learn and know His voice, we still must listen. But that is only half of it. What good is it to just be hearers of His voice, and not doers of His directions?

Have you ever been around a child of any age? If so, you know that they are most successful when they have learned not only to listen to what you have taught and instructed them to do, but more so, when they carry it out completely. We are no different.

Writing this book, writing anything, has taken me years longer than it should have out of my fear of your judgment more than any other stumbling block. I have let the fear of others' criticisms of my writing style, and even more so, my beliefs, that I have stayed silent for years! God told me to write this book back in 2012, I believe. It is 2022 y'all! The enemy is loud, and if I am not careful, I hear his voice the loudest. Worse yet, out of fear, I am prone to respond and react to him, not God.

Jonah fought a battle like mine. God gave him a noticeably clear directive to go to Nineveh and speak some pretty harsh truths to them. Who in their right minds wants to do that? Nobody, including Jonah! He wanted so much not to do what God called him to that he literally tried to run away from God.

Think we don't do that? My house has never been cleaner, and I have never served on so many committees than when I was running from writing. I told God that if He would bring me home from teaching, I would finally sit down and finish what He had started in me years ago. I am home now, and I have built my other businesses and served with more organizations than I have ever, in my life. And I have only added, maybe twenty pages. Being one million percent transparent with you, I have felt physically ill for the last few days, fully knowing the illness was my disobedience. The pain in my belly, the aching in my arm and chest was my Jonah heart, running long and hard and fast from that which God has called me to do.

Jonah had to be swallowed by a whale. I had to be brought to my knees in total brokenness. All of this just to see that I cannot outrun the hand of God. Jonah had a calling and a purpose. I have a calling and a purpose.

It is easy to believe, and I have believed, that if you ignore the call of God, it will be removed from you.

Jonah 3 tells us that the word of the Lord came upon Jonah again. As I write this, I can share with you that He has been gracious to bring His word upon me more times than should be allowed. I would have thought that he ticked a whole lot of people off when Jonah finally made it to Nineveh, challenging them to change their ways. But they did not get mad. Scripture says they received his words well, and everyone, including the king repented and fasted, begging God to relent.

I have greatly feared that I will tick off a whole lot of people when I share what God has given me to share. But I have had to learn, I am still learning, that how "they" respond to the message is between them and the one who sent it. It is my job to give it as it was given to me, not changing anything about it. Who knows how many lives it will impact, or won't? But how someone receives this message isn't what I am called to be concerned with. My calling is to write to Him alone.

What is He calling you to? Are you listening? Are you running, your Jonah heart beating clear out of your chest? It's ok. Just promise me you'll begin to slow down and listen to the thrumming of His heartbeat for you.

Father,

Please help me not to just hear Your voice but run towards it. Please do not let me be ok with just being a hearer of the word but press into me a desire to be a doer of Your word. I am so often the small child who hears Your voice but neglect the doing part. Please forgive my Jonah heart. I praise You for the incredible, unique gift to be able to hear Your voice! What a treasure You have given me to share with others. I pray for all who will hear what You have given me to say, knowing not all will hear Your voice. Be it for one person that I write this book, or for many, this book is my worship offering given for You alone.

Amen

Circumstances

As we look not to the things that are seen but to the things that are unseen. For the things that are seen are transient, but the things that are unseen are eternal.
2 Corinthians 4:18

When I first read this verse, I read, "As we look not to our circumstances, but to God. For our circumstances are temporary, but God is eternal." Sometimes, as I read the Bible, the Lord uses the gift of dyslexia to see scripture differently than it is written. I say gift because this has allowed me to see His word in a way that is personal to me. I am not rewriting the word of God. I am sharing how my brain, my heart, reads His words.

Often in life we find ourselves staring down the barrel of our circumstances and we cannot see God, our Shepherd. None of us is alone in this. We all walk through this season from one time or another. Even Peter began to sink into the crashing waves surrounding him. You see, Jesus had called him out of the boat, and he was obedient, even if hesitantly. Peter knew who his Shepherd was. He knew His voice.

Though he did not know how or why he should get out of the boat, Peter knew Who called to him. Because of who Jesus is, Peter willfully submitted to Him and stepped out of a boat, onto the water to begin walking. Peter did not just hear Jesus' voice, he went toward Him. Jesus did not call him to walk along the beach beside the water, He called Peter out of the boat, to step out onto the water. With one word, "Come." Peter went. Much like you and I, the moment he realized the gravity of his actions, he looked at the wind, the water below his feet, his circumstances, and began to submerge below the sea's surface. In his fear, Peter called to out to Jesus, his eternal Savior. He was saved.

I was thinking about Peter's boat today, seriously, over a year after writing the previous paragraph, and his boat came back into focus. I was listening to the Casting Crowns song, "Voice of Truth" and it mentions being called out of the boat, "into the realm of the unknown, where Jesus is." The boat, in that moment I realized, is every comfort zone I have ever had! Even though his boat was rocking in the midst of the wildest of stormy seas, it was his comfort zone! How often is our discomfort zone, the place we choose over embracing the "realm of the unknown, where Jesus is"?

Sometime back, I felt like God had revealed to me, that in my comfort zones, my box, I was my own god. I did not need grace. I did not need salvation. Everything was safe, controlled, planned for, and prepared for me and by me. Even though I was never going to grow in there, I was content to stay there. Oh, my old friend, contentment. Maybe contentment was the other little g god served in my little box.

Have you ever found yourself in Peter's place? Did you find yourself pleading with God, like David, to answer your prayers right away? Or did you find yourself taking control back from your Shepherd and trying to handle it on your own, staying in your boat, SS Discomfort Zone?

What we can see, feel, and experience are our temporary circumstances. Temporary though they may be, they may seem like they will never end. What we cannot see is our eternal God. He is calling us, to look beyond what we can see with our eyes, to Him who we cannot see. For what we can see is only temporary, but He is forever. He is calling us, right now, to get out of our boats, our comfort and discomfort zones, and come to Him. He is giving us the opportunity to give up our desperate attempts at control over our lives, and willfully submit to Him.

Father,

Please forgive me for all the times I have looked only at, and believed, what I could see and not what You called me to do. Help me to look to You and not the circumstances that surround me. Help me to climb out of this discomfort zone and run into your loving arms. I do not want to try to pretend I can control my life anymore. I am tired. Please help me surrender to You. Again.

Amen

He makes me lie down in green pastures.
He leads me beside still waters.
Psalms 23:2

The One Who Jesus Loved

The first time I read the words of the apostle John, I was honestly a bit put off. Irritated and judgmental might actually be a better description of my thoughts and actions. All I could think was how prideful this man was to call himself "the one who Jesus loved!" There are so many people who walk the face of the earth now and so many in John's day, too. How could one man call himself the "one" that Jesus loved? And then one day it hit me. John wasn't the prideful one at all.

John knew his identity in Christ.

John knew what most of us do not know. He was loved by Christ. He was the one who Christ loved. He was the one Christ would love so much, you could say that he loved him to death, literally. And John was not afraid to document it for the world to know then, and for all time. It wasn't pride. He knew his identity in Christ. He knew he was loved by Christ.

I, too, am the one who Jesus loved! I just have never owned it! I have never named it. I have never taken on that identity because I would have to fight my own judgements that in doing so would make me prideful.

But it isn't.

Is it prideful for me to say that I am the one my mother and father love? What about being the one my husband loves? Is that arrogant? No! Of course not! So why in the world did I think it made me uppity to realize that the creator of the universe, in the real flesh, loved me? I am still not sure I fully know. Writing a book does not make you an expert at anything. It just means you are willing to answer a calling, no matter how equipped you are, and trust me the voices of doubt have kept me from typing for too long.

Sometime back, one Sunday morning at church, I was standing along the side of the middle school cafeteria where we held church services, praying over the congregation, and rethinking this whole concept of

John, his pride not really being pride, and how he was loved by Christ. I was thanking God for showing me that I too, am like John, that I am the one Jesus loves, when the revelation kept on going.

Is Jesus the one I loved?

Read that one again. Now, read it out loud. Ouch! Come on God! Was God really asking me this? Is Jesus the one I love?

All of my life, I have sung the songs, from VBS to praise and worship services. I have written the blogs and posted the inspirational posts. I have even prayed all of the "right" prayers. But was Jesus the one I loved in all of those things? Yes, of course I loved him, and still do. Did I worship Him, and only Him? Cue the memory of my self-worship in my boat, SS Discomfort Zone.

My friend has taken several trips to India, and her observation is that the people there are worshiping gods everywhere. In all of their worshiping of many gods, she asserts that they are searching for their one true God. As our pastor pointed out Sunday, it is not just third world countries that worship many idols and false gods.

From 2003 to 2012, I carried a good bit of extra weight. I did all of the fad diets you can imagine before 2012. I took countless magic pills, vile shakes in cans, even dabbled in the oh so glamorous starvation. Anything legal, you name it, I tried it. Well, anything besides eating right and exercising. In 2012, I embarked on a long-term journey to better health. I counted every calorie, weighed myself daily (sometimes more frequently), and worked out a certain amount of time every day.

Do you notice anything about what I was doing? Sounds pretty benign right? But take a closer look. Read about my journey again. It is all about the numbers. I worshiped numbers. Numbers of calories. Numbers on scales. Numbers of minutes of exercise. Numbers on the label in the backside of my jeans. I lived and breathed and found all of my worth, in numbers. Numbers were my god.

Around 2009, I found social media. I loved sharing my little thoughts and inspirations with the world. I loved the likes and comments I would get. When Facebook updated its system to include a heart icon to show someone "loved" my posts, I was over the moon! However, when I did not get much affection for my posts, I was crushed, rejected, and left feeling irrelevant, unnecessary. It even left me doubting if I had misunderstood God about my calling to lead women in ministry. I lived, and breathed, and found my identity in the "likes" of others. Status was my god.

I cannot count, or name, the countless times that someone turned their back on me, stopped talking to me, unfriended me, on social media and in real life. The many nights I lived in the bathroom because my insides were in knots because someone was mad at me. They did not like me anymore, or I had a perceived thought that they didn't. I lived, and breathed, and found my emotional stability in the relationships I had and lost. Relationships were my god.

You still think that we do not have false idols and many gods? We bow down before money, possessions, status, weight, power, fertility, children, marriage- all of the time. Before going to the throne room of God, we bow down at the feet of these little g gods, and worship them with all of our time, talents, and treasures. Maybe you do not. But I did. Thus, why this question wrecked me.

Is Jesus the One I love?

I would love to say that I have shed all of these little g gods, and worship perfectly my one true God, all of the time, but it would be a big L Lie. I am human and sometimes struggle like all get out to make Jesus my one and only. My husband can get mad at me, and suddenly he is the one I love. Carbs take over my world, the scale seems to hate me, and suddenly numbers are the one I love. One day my social media posts seem to fall flat, and the next day they fall flat again, and suddenly approval is the one I love.

I am so thankful that though I am in pursuit of God, my Shepherd, desperately straining toward my one true God, He loves me even when I fall short. But this lavish gift of grace does not give me permission to willfully make these mistakes and choices. It does, however, give undeserved grace when I have fallen.

I am certainly the one who Jesus loves, and I am so thankful that I am. And you, Beloved, are the one Jesus loves. I pray that by seeing the countless ways He has showered me with His love and grace, you will know that your perfectly imperfect life is not out of the reach of His love and grace. You, my friend, cannot screw up that big. You are not that powerful. Isn't that a reassuring thought? So, keep striving to hear His voice, always trying to advance closer to Him. He wants to be the one and only that I love, that you love. And when we get to Glory one day, He will finally be our one and only love.

Are there any little g gods that you struggle with? Have you ever obsessed about something to the point it almost seemed like worship? Have you overcome these things and found victory? You still working through this season? It is humbling to admit my massive failures, but I pray that in doing so, it speaks grace to you, grace that reaches to a season of life you have yet to glimpse.

Father,

Please forgive me for the numerous times I have sought after so many loves that were not You. Thank You for the grace you shed for my many flaws and sins. I pray that You will never allow me to be comfortable in worshiping anything above or below You. Please never let me settle for anything less than Your love. I do love You so, and I praise You!

Amen

Still Waters

When I read about being led by still waters, so many images pop up. The image that resonates most with me, and what I penned next to this specific verse in my Bible, "a mirror". A mirror. Perfectly still water reflects images with perfect clarity. I believe God brings us along still waters to bring us to a place of self-reflection. I believe that He brings us to still waters to show us who we are in Him. Remember, the one Jesus loves?

Now, throw a pebble in the water and what happens to what was once perfectly clear? The ripples distort the mirrored image, making all difficult to discern. Some seasons are glorious and even when one pebble makes a few ripples, things tend to return to smooth with great ease. These days, it seems most of us are walking along whitewater rapids. There is no clarity to be found. We can no longer look into the water and see ourselves looking back, let alone the work of Christ in our lives. But, come alongside a water body that has learned its place and purpose, and you too, will begin to see your place and purpose.

What is the water like in your world today? I really want you to stop and, pun intended, reflect. In this exact season of life, what can you see of your identity in Christ as it is reflected in these waters? As I write that question, I feel strongly that I must say that though the waters may be choppy due to chaos in your life, your identity in Christ may still be crystal clear to you. I believe that you can be firm in your identity, even when your world is far from still and calm. I think it is also important to note that even when the waters are distorted, your identity can be solidified in Him. A shaken reflection due to circumstances does not mean a shaken identity in Him.

These still waters are a place where I see Christ, our great Shepherd, leading us to see ourselves better. It is easy, especially in the hard times, to get into the blame game when we start to reflect. I could blame this person or that, for the pain that has ruttered my ship for too long, but it does not change the fact that I am solely responsible for me and for my own actions. In these still waters of reflection, I begin to see me with the kind of clarity that only a Savior can provide. I must dig deep to find the courage to look into these waters and allow myself to see the woman looking back at me. She needs me to be open and allow the Holy Spirit to work within me. And reflection is the beginning of the journey.

He leads me beside still waters. He leads. He doesn't yank me along. He does not force Himself upon me. He leads. He is a gentleman. You could say, He guides me beside still waters. Do you hear what I hear? He shepherds us beside still waters. How beautiful is that idea? Our Shepherd brings us to still waters, a safe place to reflect on who He is and who we are - the one who Jesus loves.

Father,

What a beautiful scenery You have painted for us. A place of tranquility, a place where water knows what it's purpose is, so that You can do a work in and through us. Thank You for taking us to a place where You can show us who we are in You. Thank You for loving us!

Amen

The Wall Between Mirrors

The not so glamorous world of entrepreneurship means a life full of networking meetings. One morning I had an exceptionally early meeting which meant getting up even earlier to get ready. I was about ready to go when I decided to use my tiny compact mirror to look at the back of my hair, to make sure I had gotten it all with the straightener. When I first held up the tiny mirror in front of me, all I saw was the wall behind me. You see, I have two mirrors, with space between them, over our two sinks in the master bath. When I first held up the mirror, I was standing between them, thus I could not see my reflection.

So why am I writing about the wall between my mirrors? Well, because I needed a reflection to tell me the state of my hair and I had not positioned myself in front of one. In life, we, I, need a mirror to reflect the truth about the state of things in my life.

Can I be very real for a moment? I struggle greatly with allowing women into my life to be the much needed mirrors I need for pointing me back to God's truth. I know how to be vulnerable, but I struggle to allow myself to be in close, committed friendships. I know many of the reasons why, though I haven't the space to net them all out here. Regardless of the reasons, I sometimes still find myself, positioned in front of walls, not mirrors, when I most need their truthful reflection.

These "walls" in life, are the friends who tell you what they think you want to hear. "You deserve…" "He doesn't deserve…" "You shouldn't have to…" These friends feel like they are giving you exactly what you need, but they aren't. They are not reflecting anything. They are dull, and not at all reflective of the Lord within you.

Whether you call them a circle of friends or a tribe, you need mirrors, not walls. I need them. These are the people who we give intimate (not sexual) access to us, and beautifully reflect the truths about us we sometimes cannot see, or maybe do not want to see. Unlike walls, who reflect nothing, these "mirrors" will sometimes reflect an extremely uncomfortable truth. Sometimes it will feel great to hear what they say, as they affirm what the Spirit has grown in you. I strongly suggest that these mirrors are the same gender as yourself so as to avoid the confusion of intimacy of friends, over the intimacy of lovers.

I am incredibly thankful for the countless women who have patiently endured this battle with me and have not given up on our friendship. I am thankful for the women who were willing to be mirrors, speaking truth to me, in love, when needed. I am so appreciative that they allowed the Lord to speak in and through them. I know that saying the hard stuff, is just that, hard. But still, they obeyed, and it gave life to me in countless ways and in countless seasons.

I wish that I could say that I am always willing to be someone's still waters. Being this level of honest is painfully uncomfortable for me. Remember the very real struggle with people pleasing? It is not an easy job being someone else's mirror. I cannot give enough praise to the Lord for bringing me alongside women who were willing to do the hard stuff, say the truthful things, and be the still waters I desperately needed throughout various seasons in my life.

Take a moment of reflection here, in the mirror of this text, and pray. Ask God to show you who is around you? Who pops into your mind? Take note of whom you have allowed to be a mirror and who you are around that is only a nonreflective, textured wall. Is one group more prevalent than the other? Do you need to pray for more godly influences in your life? Do you need to rise up and be more of a godly influence to others? How many people are counting on you to be a mirror and not seeking you to be a wall?

Come alongside this still water with your Shepherd and let Him show you what He needs you to see. I pray you pry open your heart to receive what He is trying to share with you this day.

Father,

I praise You that You saw fit not to leave me as I was, but rather chose to surround me with still waters and mirrors, rather than walls. It hasn't always felt good to reflect on myself and do the work You have called me to do within myself, but I praise Your plan and purpose for it all. I pray that You will continue to grow me as a mirror, that I would not fear the rejection that sometimes accompanies truth. Your love and approval is all I need and will ever need. Please do not ever let me be comfortable accepting anything else than Your approval.

Amen

My name is Bryn, and I am a striver.

"Be still and know that I am God." Psalm 46:10

"Be still" This phrase makes me think of two seemingly different things right off the bat. One thing it makes me think of is my fourth child, at the ripe old age of squirmy three-year-old little boy, and the second thing that comes to mind are the words "quit striving!" But are they really all that different?

Now, let us take a look at another scripture. One where we see that God calls us to have faith like a child, and if I remember correctly, Lord, aren't three-year-olds kind of squirmy? And doesn't striving mean to work hard to achieve something?

All of this totally makes me think of a toddler who knows there are cookies high up on a shelf in the pantry. Can you see the tot clumsily scaling each shelf, the silverware drawer pulled to its absolute most stretched position, tiny toes gripping, determined to get said box? Nothing gets in the way of this small child and the sugary goodness just out of reach. They will work to no end to reach the goal they have set out to achieve, knocking down box after box, can after can. I'm thinking that, "*Be still and know that I am God.*" is kind of like addressing a squirmy three-year-old on a mission! I suppose that might mean I might just be that squirmy three-year-old on my own mission. And now, You are telling me to be still?

Scripture says to "be still", not act, not strive, not work harder, but to be still. At first glance, this direction is seemingly passive. But in all uncomfortable truth, this direction is quite active.

It is ridiculously hard to be still when my world is falling apart, in fact it is the very last thing I want to do. I want to take all things into my own, very incapable hands, and fix them. Being still requires that I wait for His timing, not rely on my own. Being still means not scaling the side of my circumstances, fully grown toes desperately clinging to my own ability, trying to achieve what I think is best from my limited view of the world.

Which brings me to the latter part of the same scripture:

"and know that I am God."

He is God. I am not. Close the book, we can stop right here, right? It's that easy right? Not even a chance. God is calling us to stop striving and know that He alone is the one in control. He's got it. It may not make sense in the slightest, but He's got it. He knows the beginning of time to the end of it, and my blink-of-an-eye chapter somewhere in the midst of it. He knows every detail, to the minutia and how it all needs to work together for His glory. His glory, not my happiness. Do not miss that. There are whole books written on this topic. So, for the sake of not ending up writing a book within a book, let us leave it here: He is God. I am not.

When I do the opposite of what the Word tells me to do, and I am busy, trying to control all of the outcomes and predict and stress over the future, nothing goes as planned. I find myself worn out from the journey, wondering where God is, the very same God who holds me by my right hand and never lets go. The exact same God who would hide me in a cleft to protect me, allowing me only to see Him in reflection. I indulge in defeated thoughts of why a "good" God would allow such bad things to happen, even though I know it is at my own striving hands that I have arrived at this place.

But when I am still, when I allow my Shephard to lead me beside still waters, He is God, and I can see a perfect reflection of who I am, the one who Jesus loves.

I love this marriage of the 23rd and 46th Psalm and the words that jump off the page from between the lines, and into my heart.

"He makes me lie down in green pastures." (23rd Psalm)
Rest.
"Be still." (46th Psalm)
Stop striving.

Quit trying so hard.

Quit worshiping false gods.

"He leads me beside still waters." (23rd Psalm)

Know your identity.

Know your purpose.

Know your place.

"And know that I am God." (46th Psalm)

Know He is God alone.

You are not.

I think it is important not to blow right past the differences between stillness and stagnation.

The stillness of the waters we are led to and by, are waters of reflection and nourishment. They are waters that have flowed down from the heights and have beheld the beauty and glory of God from the mountain top. Still waters are the perfect place for the growth of the soul. These are the waters that feed the places the world tries to leave parched and malnourished. They are the waters that now sit in a pool because they know their place. They know that in stillness, we can reflect and behold the image of our Creator.

In contrast, stagnant waters are full of disease. Take a look at the word "disease." Dis-ease. Dis means not or no. It literally means no ease. Isn't that exactly what disease causes? These waters have stopped moving. These once mobile waters have ceased to move and have created the perfect environment for stagnation. They have refused to be used for their original purpose. They are places of murky, distorted, reflections. Stagnant waters can be distracting, because they too are still. The difference is that you can never go to stagnant waters for nourishment. You will come to these places desperate for living water and surely leave worse than when you came. These are the waters that starve the soul. These are the waters that starve a life.

Being still, this very active command is not an easy one for any of us to follow. Knowing He alone is God, is also quite the challenge at times. Remember the many little g gods we battle with daily? The beautiful thing is that

His grace is there when we strive, when we are restless to control things again, when we do not surrender to His timing over our own. There is grace when we try to take His role from Him and try to be our own king. And we find this grace, when we allow Him to lead us alongside still waters, and we rest. We receive Him.

Father,

It is incredibly hard not to try to control things. I have no clue when You are going to finally act and do what I think You should do, or if You will at all. I pray that you will show me when I am looking for Your direction in stagnant waters. I need more of You, and so much less of me. Lead me, Father.

Amen

Season of Rest

In 2012, I became extremely ill with a mystery illness. No blood test or scan could figure out what was wrong with me, but I will tell you, I lived as though I was preparing to die. I was lethargic to say the least. I felt unwell most of the time, running low grade fevers often. My husband and children had to carry my load for over a year and a half. It was in that season that the Lord showed me that I must rest. Not only did He suggest I rest, but He also left me no choice.

Isaiah 30:15 says,

> "For thus says the Lord, the Holy One of Israel, 'In returning and rest you shall be saved; in quietness and in trust shall be your strength.' But you were unwilling."

When I read this, I internalized this as to not rest is to sin. "Unwilling" that is not something I want God to use when describing me. Oh, that I had seen this verse sooner! I fought the very rest that was being gifted to me. I had no idea that I would need this rest for the mountain I was about to move. The mountain that was just out of sight, yet right ahead of me. I would need this precious gift of rest to recuperate from the mountains I had just cleared in the decade behind me. Why didn't I see it before? I needed to allow my Shepherd to lead me beside still waters of reflection, to know I was beyond spent from the battles fought, and not ready for the battles to come.

Some time back, my husband parted ways with his most recent job. He wore himself out, day in and day out, driving here and there, taking countless calls from staff and ownership, constantly mediating customer, and staff relations. He never realized he was keeping such a frenetic pace until it all came to a stop on January 1st.

The law of inertia states: an object at rest stays at rest and an object in motion stays in motion with the same speed and in the same direction unless acted upon by an unbalanced force. Scott was moving, at full speed, and a very unbalanced force pushed back and caused him to stop. Scott found himself, this year, in the very same place that I had been in 2012. He found himself arriving at the doorstep of rest, having never chosen to make the journey there.

Now, I do not know about the world that you live in, but if it is anything like any of the roads I have walked, it is a blur of faces and events, blindly rushing by, yet all begging for your full attention. Someone, no everyone, in your family needs to be everywhere, at the same time, including yourself and there is only one of you to do it all. And yet, in all of this busyness, there is a command to rest. This divinely inspired directive to rest may remind you of another scripture we talked about previously, to "be still." Yeah, we haven't quite put that one to rest. Pun very much intended.

There is something about being still. Being still means giving up something. Something you and I and everyone else have in limited quantity. It is the sacrifice of time. Time that you could spend doing laundry, getting groceries, sitting in a carpool line, working out, attending the umpteenth game this month. It means putting down the phone and giving up the battle within to scroll mindlessly, while precious time wastes away.

Allowing the Lord, the Shepherd of your heart and life, to lead you beside still waters, allowing Him to reveal to you more about yourself and Him, requires you to be still. It requires a sacrifice of intentionality. Having an encounter with the Creator of the Universe can happen in a moment, out of absolutely nowhere. But, having a relationship with Him, that takes time and intentionality. It takes being still. It takes rest.

Can you imagine if all you ever had, to connect you and your mate, were random happenstance moments, neither of you being intentional about pursuing a relationship with the other? Relationships take purposeful time investments. When Scott and I met, it was a whirlwind marathon of long phone calls, long talks on my mother's couch, and dates, lots of dates.

After three whole months of knowing each other, we married and soon after realized we had no idea who we had married. We have spent the last twenty-six years learning about each other. Some time back, I learned that he does not like corn. Who doesn't like corn?! This random encounter with him, learning he doesn't like corn, isn't what bonded us and solidified our relationship, though I will tell you it through me for a loop! What built our relationship were the long, drawn out fights that forced down deep roots, the late-night pillow talks that watered the soil of our dreams, the sacrifices made all along the way that pruned away the dead parts of our old lives, making room for the new that God would create in and through us. It was the intentional time investment that made our marriage relationship what it is today.

My relationship, your relationship, with God, is no different. It is worthy to say again, you can have random, incredible encounters with God, but having a relationship with Him will require intentional time and sacrifice.

Why do I bring all of this up? Let's go back to the verse and title of this chapter, *"He makes me lie down in green pastures, He leads me beside still waters."* The very first thing, in this verse, the Psalmist points out about the Shepherd of his life, He makes him lie down in green pastures.

Rest.

His Shepherd makes him lie down. He makes him rest. He does not suggest that David should take a nap if he has time after he has finished all of his kingly duties. He does not recommend, on the latest royal blog, that a little shuteye would do him some good. No, the Bible actually says that *"He makes me lie down..."* God knew from the beginning of time that we would need rest. Genesis 2:2 says:

"And on the seventh day God finished his work that he had done, and he rested on the seventh day from all his work that he had done."

Newsflash to the twenty something I was when I first saw this as an adult- God was not tired! God is not human. He does not grow weary. He rested on the seventh day so that we would know that we should, too. God so loved us that he would show us that He can do more with His hands in six days, than we can do with our hands in seven.

So, we have to rest. But take a look at the second half of that first sentence, "...*in green pastures.*" One of my favorite things to do as a child, when the world didn't need one million master planned communities, was to lay in the middle of a field, cushioned by the lush green grass, and stare at the blank blue canvas above me. I could see His glory in creation from horizon to horizon. I wish my children could have the luxury of seeing the same unobstructed view.

In the world of botany, green is the color of a living plant. Green pastures are alive! They are teeming with life, in fact. Making me lie down, in green pastures, is a beautiful way for me to surrender my will to His will for my emotional and physical health, as well as surrounding me with the fully alive creation around me. Life gives birth to life. Lying in lush green grass, does something life-giving for the soul, and quite possibly life-limiting for the sinuses if you have allergy issues.

So, is He saying to you, to me, that we need to lay down in the middle of nowhere and rest? Maybe, but I do not think so. I really think in my heart of hearts that this is where He shows me that I need to rest in His Word. This is where He is leading me to be intentional about spending time with Him, getting to know Him better, building an incredible, trusting, faith-filled relationship with Him. This is where I relax, and I breathe, and I let my walls down, learning more about who He is and who He says that I am. This is where I choose to put down my phone and all that the world fights to tell me that I am, where I choose to silence the voices that clamor from the depths of that stagnant water, and I strain to hear His still, small voice.

Life gives birth to life.

Resting in the lush, green, life-giving pastures of His Word, restores my weary world-ravaged soul. I need it more than I want to admit, and He knows it. That is why He *makes* me lie down in green pastures. He knows my heart and how it restlessly strives and struggles as a squirmy child. He knows that I am better fit for the battle of my life, when I am well rested in His well-proved Word.

Father,

Please help me to seek Your Word about the word of man. It is so easy for me to fall into this. Each time I succumb to the approval and words of others, I worn out. But each time I come to You, and rest in Your Word, I walk away fulfilled and faith filled. Oh, that knowing would keep me from the snares of man, but many times over it does not. Please help me. Please forgive me.

Amen

He restores my soul.
He leads me in paths of
righteousness for his name's sake.

Psalms 23:3

Leaves

In my former bedroom, there was an answered prayer- a window seat. I have long wanted one of these little safe havens. I would say that I have yearned for this since I was a little girl. As a thirty-seven, almost thirty-eight-year-old woman, I finally had one of my own.

One early October afternoon, as I sat in my little planter box, I watched the wind as it began to pick up and a few leaves started to fall. And as I sat there, a word came to me:

The winds have to howl, and the rain has to pour, and gravity must tug hard for the leaves to fall. And the leaves must fall if the tree is to be reborn in the Spring. It must lose all that it is, and all that it has, and even appear as though it has lost its very life, if it is to gain it again in the Spring.

I feel like these words were so critical to me because the Fall season, leading into the Winter season, is always so difficult for me.

First of all, I am a sunflower soul. Do you know what I mean when I say this? I need copious amounts of sunshine, and it seems as though Fall and Winter seem to be allergic to anything related to sunshine. The days get shorter and shorter, and the nights seem to go on for days. 5:00pm becomes the new midnight and all I seem to be able to do is embrace all of this godly rest I am supposed to have. When all I really want is to be outside and energetic, I cannot seem to shake the dark and endless exhaustion.

My worst struggles with deep darkness come in these months. I need sunshine and warmth, both in copious supply.

I have watched how life appears to come in seasons that change as well. Changes that are not always invited in for dinner but show up regardless, and almost always overstay their welcome. Does anyone really like life change, especially the change that we are required to make within our own selves? What about the undesired change that comes with a loved one's new changes?

One of the darkest Winter seasons of my life, was when Scott had fallen back into his addiction. It was the worst bout of it I had experienced with him in his almost decade long battle. His intentional changes forced my hand. This meant, that I too, had to change. I had to react and respond to his changes. I could not be the same. My world, our world, could not just carry on as it previously was lived. My life was forever changed because of his changes.

I was angry. I was resentful. I was let down. I did not choose this change in directions, in seasons. I did not ask for this. I was not the one choosing this path. I did not want to have to step up while he stepped away. But my, let me rephrase that, *our* children needed present parents, so one of us had to do it and this unwanted change in him mandated that it had to be me and me alone, most of the time.

But God.

As always with our Savior and Shepherd, something uncomfortably beautiful happened during that season of life. God showed me, in the still waters of reflection, that I too, was fighting my own addictions.

Wait! What?!

I wasn't addicted!

This thought did not sit well with me. I remember very well when this moment first hit me. I was taking a nap, or at the very least, trying to rest while five restless little ones fought much needed sleep all around me in our emotionally empty, king-sized bed. Didn't they know what a sin it is not to nap, I mean rest, or at least listen and obey their worn out, stressed out momma?

Nap or no nap, God was right there with me. The thoughts turned over and over in my head, as I tossed about, desperately chasing sleep and running from His uncomfortable, inconvenient truth. He was with me in my bed, my thoughts, His truth, and my addiction.

I was addicted, painfully addicted. My drug of choice was food, more specifically, I was addicted to eating large quantities of food and fast. The faster I ate, the more I could consume before my body began to ache from the swelling of my stomach. In my emotional emptiness, I tore through food quickly so as not to experience the feeling of fullness from food.

I would binge and binge, and never purge. A problem I realized later, had started around the age of ten. Food had long been more than my comfort; it was my drug. I felt I was entitled to food and loads of it, all at once. Food was a little g god I had picked up along the way, and the fuller the belly the better the high.

Scott knew that he could bribe me with my favorite goodies. He knew my weakness for greasy foods and various sweets. I could be bought with food, and my health showed it. Oh, that makes me ill, even today, to type and reread those words.

I could be bought with food.

God really netted it out for me.

Oh, how I argued with God about this.

"Scott's addiction is stealing our money from us."

To which the reply I heard in my heart was,

"So is yours."

"But Scott's addiction is hurting his health. His addiction could kill him!"

"So could yours."

"But Scott's addiction is destroying our marriage and tearing our family apart."

"So is yours."

In that day, I could see that addiction, is addiction, is addiction. It was time I looked in the mirror and face the woman I had become. I had to look my addiction in the face. I had to grow. I had to change. I had to "get sober". Our children needed parents, and though neither of us wanted to do all that it would take to get free from our own addictions, one of us had to face them head-on.

Let me be the very first to say in this moment, change is not easy, nor is it usually desired. In my case, and maybe even yours, it is not even always solicited. But it is necessary.

In the still waters of my attempted nap that day, God showed me a very real work that needed to be done in my soul. He revealed to me that I needed the full restoration of my mind, my body, and my soul. I could not continue life this way, but I did not know how to stop what I was doing. I did not know how to stop overeating. I did not know how to exercise or move my morbidly overweight body. I did not know how to persevere when things would become hard, and my life was a series of painful challenges. Though I did not know how to stop these things, I knew how to quit on myself, and sadly, I was really good at it. Quitting was easy.

Beginning the necessary overhaul of my whole world was hard, since food had been my comfort from an incredibly young age. Work hard and earn good grades? Let's celebrate by eating out! Had a bad day at school? Ice cream will catch your tears! Even following great workouts, I felt entitled to a hearty, greasy meal as my congratulations! Let me pause and make this abundantly clear, my mom is an amazing woman and an even more amazing mom. She has always been a hero in my life. What I learned about relationships with food, was entirely what she caught growing up. All that she did, she did in love.

I remember the day I met with a personal trainer for the first time. I was twenty-seven. I drove for almost an hour to get to her house. We had connected through Craigslist. She was looking for a housekeeper to trade cleaning for trainer services. This was perfect because I was a maid, putting myself through college! I was so excited about this appointment. At two hundred and thirty pounds, I was the largest I had ever been, yet too small for any weight loss television show to give me a chance. I needed help. I was desperate for help and this was my chance to get it.

I really felt like all was going well in the consultation until she said that I needed to set up a rewards system for when I achieved the weight loss goals, she believed I could reach. I knew right away what I would want for my first reward. I thought a cheat meal would be exactly what I deserved. This was where I ran, like a herd of turtles, right into defeat. She shattered my bubble when she said it had to be a nonfood reward. I was literally stumped, like, I had no idea what other kinds of rewards there were out there. I had never rewarded myself before without it being food related. After the consultation, we worked out for a little while.

Like, I shared with you earlier, I was an absolute expert at quitting on myself. And I did just that. I never went back to her again. I did not call. I did not explain. I walked away, super sore I might add, back into the deep darkness. I hid and continued to feed my addiction to food. No goals achieved. No nonfood rewards given. Just me, binging in the welcoming arms of my addiction.

I would love to tell you that the restoration process was an easy one, or even slightly glamorous. But it was not. Regardless, I had to get healthy for me, and for my family. The Lord had already shown me that my addiction was stealing money from our family, was hurting my health and could kill me, and was hurting my relationships.

It was several more years before I finally surrendered my addiction to food. Even after Scott found his sobriety, I was still badly struggling, fighting against mine. I was motivated that he had a date that he could celebrate his sobriety every year, May 1st. Until the day that I laid it down, all I had was nothing but failed attempts at extreme fad diets and briefly attempted exercise programs.

In the beginning of my restoration, I was angry and resentful at Scott most of the time. Everything in my flesh wanted to continue to eat the way I had always eaten and just hope and pray over my food: "Lord, bless *this food to the nourishment of my body.*" Have you ever thought about what you are asking the Creator of the Universe to do? "*Lord, please turn this cheeseburger and large fries and large, sweet tea into a salad without dressing or croutons in my body. Please?*" What nourishment did I think He was going to do inside my body with the materials I was putting in it? This isn't a water into wine situation.

Scott has always been drawn to a healthier way of eating. Honestly, I kind of resented him for this, for literally years of our marriage. He never really liked my greasy food way of life, but he put up with it for a long time to make me happy. His health suffered greatly, just to appease my appetite. He put on over one hundred and thirty pounds from the time we met.

Once I began the process of trying to reclaim my health, Scott started wanting me to eat vegetables! Seriously, who asks someone they love to eat those things? Restaurants are in on this too, but one step worse. They want you to pay more for a bowl of vegetables. They call it a salad, they charge you a steep price, and you can bet that you will be hungry in an hour or so. I just couldn't. Who wastes that kind of money and on food they don't even want to eat, and certainly will not feel in about an hour?

But I did. I ate vegetables. I even learned I liked broccoli and cauliflower. I learned that I liked salads with chicken and cheese and pickles. Weird, I know, but hey, if it gets you to eat the overpriced bowl of veggies, add those pickles in! I had to find what worked and somewhere along the way, I discovered healthy foods that I liked.

Then came the time to address the overeating. This was my all binge, no purge, eating disorder of choice. I was, and sometimes still struggle with being, a binge eater. This goes way back to food being my comfort. A big heart ache equates to even bigger portions. I ran to the throne of oversized meals over any other source for emotional support. Switching from a footlong sandwich, chips, and a drink, to a six-inch sub and water was genuine torture. I am quite sure I was convinced that I was going to starve to death, and I am fairly certain Scott got to hear about it much and often.

I learned along the way that a root cause of my overeating came from poverty. Though in our married life there was never a missed meal, I ate as though I thought there might be. In retrospect, I realize I did not trust God for my next meal, so I ate enough for several meals in one.

Think back to childhood. Did you ever hear the phrase, "Make sure you clean your plate?" Yep. Me too. "Don't waste food." "Don't leave food on your plate." These scripts kept the spoon dutifully in my hand, shoveling in bite after bite, long after my belly ached from fullness. Better to ache from fullness than emptiness, I thought. The burden of leaving anything on my plate is still heavy. I still struggle with the battle between wasting those last couple of bites, or just choking them down so that I am not squandering the gift of the meal

I have been given. "There are children starving all over the world." Script 1,001 reminds me. Side note- I very much said all of these to my children, too.

With time, and perseverance with better choices, the weight started coming off. As I stated earlier in the study, this is when I began to worship numbers. Numbers of calories in my food, the numbers on the scale I stepped on countless times a day, and the numbers in my clothing. I wanted to achieve all of the success, have the health transformation I so desperately needed, and under it all, I knew I wanted to have all of the glory. After all, I was the one doing all of the work, right? No, even in that season of physical restoration, God was doing a new thing in my spirit, for His glory and not my own.

> *"Behold, I am doing a new thing; now it springs forth, do you not perceive it? I will make a way in the wilderness and rivers in the desert." Isaiah 43:19*

One of the darkest, driest, wilderness times in my life, was sadly while I was well on my journey to an emotionally and physically healthier me. I ran across an old scripture that screamed volumes to me. It shouted what I did not want to hear. It held me accountable for behavior I did not want to own. It made me face the truth in my actions, the actions that held me captive in the dark.

Romans 8:6 says,

"For to set the mind on the flesh is death, but to set the mind on the spirit is life and peace."

This passage gashed a hole into my continued darkness and shined light on my self-worship. In an effort to lose weight, I lost sight of why I was losing weight. I became so fixated on myself, at some point, that I forgot that I was on this journey to share it with others.

See, God had already shown me that by walking this difficult road ahead of me, I would have a unique hope to offer others. Others in the same situation as me. I would have a hope to offer others who had no hope that healing and restoration could happen. Hope that eating vegetables, exercising, and nonfood rewards are good and necessary, for the body and soul.

The numbers I worshiped were everywhere and I let them define me in a way I no longer allowed God to. If I woke up and I had gained any weight, I was worthless, in my mind. If I woke up and the numbers were in my favor, I was edified again. Down, and further down my spirit went. I had lost sight of His truth and purpose and had found my way down into a deep, dark cave, where I was my own self-carved idol and free to worship my own carved image.

It is easy for me to isolate from others. Cave-dwelling is what my family and I call it. It is something I can do in the presence of a huge crowd, or in my living room with just my family. In this part of my journey, I isolated from all life that I knew. I went to work, spent time with my family, and continued fixating on losing weight. I justified my behaviors by noticing and proclaiming that body builders also must think about all of the nutrients, numbers, and have prepped food always with them. And they are the epitome of healthy, right?

What I did not know was that this cave I was hiding in, this fixation on getting healthy and trying to find new life, was really much more. It was a spiritual grave. The scripture said to focus on my flesh was death, and it was. It was my main focus day in and day out, until He showed me what I was doing.

I remember I was in the middle of worship, on a Thursday night at church, when God showed me the spiritual grave I was hiding in. My so-called safe place, my cave, had been transformed into a grave when I ceased to live, and operate in the purpose He had for me. I was hiding from the world, from God, but more than that, I was dying spiritually while becoming more alive physically.

In that gross, dark moment, I made a declaration that I was running out of that grave and not looking back. I had to focus on Him alone, if I wanted to find freedom again, if I wanted to find life in Him again. I had to tear down the erected idol I had made of myself and leave it and the cave behind me.

That night, in the midst of a foggy, dimly lit sanctuary, I begged for forgiveness, for worshiping myself, for worshiping my progress, and for running from Him and His plans for me. I pleaded for His mercy for making any of this about me and my glory. His grace was and still is abounding! He has revealed to me how this moment of brokenness, and all of the other moments along this journey, are for His glory and not my own. Even though I was, and admittedly still can be, a total mess, in my victories, He gets the glory. A beautiful thing happens when I can offer this hope and help someone else to walk through their own season. The peace He has given me, frees me not to be obsessed with the progress and defined by the numbers, but rather be restored and made new, defined by Him and for His glory and His purpose.

Have you been there my sweet friend? In the dark and dank cave, hiding from your life, hiding from your purpose, worshiping the temple, rather than the One dwelling within the temple? Are you there now? Yeah, I know, admitting that feels gross and terrifying. I know very well how scary it is to come out of the cave, when hiding seems so safe. But can I share with you, ever so gently, staying in the cave is not safer. It is not a stronghold of protection. It isn't the cleft of the rock with His loving hand over the edge. It is a tomb. It is an empty grave.

The good news is, the very same One who rolled away the stone meant to keep Jesus in, is the very same One who rolled away the stone meant to keep me in, to keep you in. He's kind of this cool Holy Roller if you will.

When you finally see your cave for what it is, you can come out and begin the process of healing. And you know what is even more beautiful than your own freedom? Helping others to find their own freedom, through the unique hope that only you can give them, just by walking out of your own cave and allowing Him to work in you!

Blessed be the God and Father of our Lord Jesus Christ, the Father of mercies and God of all comfort, who comforts us in all our affliction, so that we may be able to comfort those who are in any affliction, with the comfort with which we ourselves are comforted by God.
2Corinthians 1:3-4

Friend, will you allow Him to roll away the stone? Will you come out and begin the process of healing whatever it is that has held you captive? I pray you will. Your hope has so much power that this hurting world needs. His purpose for your life, it is greatly needed. You are needed. Will you allow Him to shine light in the darkness? I know it is scary, but I am right here with you. He is right there with you. You are not alone in this battle. You never will be. When the world walks away, He is still there, loving you.

Father,

Thank You for not letting me sit in the darkness. Thank You for calling me into Your glorious light of truth. You knew I was not ok. You knew what I was doing that was robbing me of life. You even knew that I did not know what damage I was doing to my own self by keeping my eyes on my flesh. I thought getting healthy was the answer, but what I was doing was not healthy at all. Thank You for the thousandth time for forgiving me.

I love You so!

Amen

To this day, I cannot name the day that this happened. And to be honest, the day does not mean what I thought it would. What has value is the deliverance that only He could do in my life. My addiction to food would still be keeping me in chains if not for His salvation and redemption of my life. Had He not challenged me to see that it was an addiction to begin with, I would be in bondage today.

I have learned that I do not have to know the exact day that I found freedom. It turns out, there were many days that I found freedom: the day I surrendered my addiction, the day I overcame overeating, the day I embraced exercise, and the day I ran out of the grave I had isolated into. I found freedom from my own self. I am praying for you to find whatever freedoms He is calling you to.

Restoration

In my Bible, next to the words of the third verse of the twenty-third Psalm, I wrote the word, "restoration". Up to this point in this chapter of the Bible, the Shepherd is revealing who He is, what His role is, and who we are. He is taking us on a journey of self-reflection, and we are beginning to see the importance of taking a deeper look into our own selves. This hard work is for the birds, as my folks would say, but it is a worthy work.

As we have journeyed in this direction, you have seen some of my grossest battles. Had He not brought me through this process of reflection, led me alongside still waters, I would never have made it to the next step of restoration. I must know who He is and who I am, before I can begin to allow Him to restore me to that which He created and called me to be, the disciple Jesus who loves.

As you have travelled this road with me thus far, have you just read the words, or has something begun to stir within you? Are you speed reading, catching every few words? Are you reading just so that you can say you read for girl group on Sunday night?

Friend, I hope with all that is in me, that you are taking your time and digesting each word. I pray that our heavenly Father is softening your heart to receive just who He says He is and who He says He is not. Please hear my heart, I do not want you to take my word for it. The words you have read are the descriptions and encounters I have had with my Shepherd. They are personally mine. I hate to be crass, but they aren't yours for the taking. Who He is and who He reveals Himself to be, to uniquely you, will only be revealed to you through your own digging and personal investment of time. May you glean hope from my story, but His truth from His story.

I sincerely pray that you are allowing Him to lead you alongside still waters of reflection and rest. I pray that whatever He is stirring within you, you are listening to, no matter how uncomfortable it may be to process. Better yet, are you sharing these thoughts you are processing through with your group, or with someone you trust? Are you acknowledging them to yourself? It is easy to keep running from His prompting, and difficult to sit with and attend to His direction. But, sweet friend, I promise, it is worth it.

Maybe your road is similar to mine and life-giving hope is found on each page. If God could restore a salad avoiding, self-worshiping woman like me, there is hope for you. Maybe you are the person I have kept going for. Maybe you are the one who He loves so much that He would call me to conquer food and fears and dare greatly to write my words out loud for. This is one of the scariest and most humbling things I have ever done, but hear me say this out loud, YOU ARE WORTH IT! Yes, I just yelled a little bit, but it kind of needed to be done. You alone are one million percent worth overcoming fears of rejection and criticism. You are worth hours in the gym and miles on the road. You are worth learning how to eat again. You are worth running out of the tomb I had buried myself in. You are worth every torn down, carved image I made of myself. You are worth it.

But maybe you and I have totally different stories. Maybe your pain is indescribable and working on yourself, when your life is what it is, because of the hands of another person's careless choices, is the last thing you want to do, and you feel justified in believing you should not have to. I do get that too. I hear your pain, and I thank you for allowing me to hold your heart for a moment.

Have you let anyone into this pain with you? Does someone know that your world looks like this right now? In a season like this, Satan wants nothing more than to separate you from the flock by whispering lies in your ear. He will tell you that no one wants to hear about your "drama". He will tell you that everyone is too busy to come help you and you are a burden to all who actually do help you. He is so deceptive that you won't necessarily know that he has cut you off from all who love you and want to take the other oar to your boat.

Have no doubt, the Lord loves you so much that He has sent people into your life to walk with you in this very specific moment. Please let them give you their gift of time and resources. You are not alone. If you do not see them right now, please pray for Him to begin to reveal them to you.

Wherever you find yourself, this is your cross-roads my friend. This is where you decide whether you will allow the Holy Spirit to move through these words and into your heart, or you decide to close the book and chalk it up to more words from a "self-help know it all" who knows nothing at all, but her own stories and some Bible verses she must have looked up and shared out of context.

I get it.

I have made both choices.

But this is not about my choice. I have made my choices. This is about you. Do you need to go back and intentionally reread? Did you skim over the words to get through it? Did you drink up each word? Have you allowed a friend into this with you? Restoration is here for the taking. Will you do the work? Will you be led by your Shepherd by the still waters of reflection? Will you allow yourself to rest in the life-giving green pastures of His Word? Will you allow yourself to begin to see yourself as the one who Jesus loves?

He was leading me down an extremely uncomfortable path toward righteousness, for His name's sake, not my own. The journey to greater physical and spiritual health had nothing to do with me at all. It had to do with a unique hope that could only be born out of the process.

The unique hope you and I receive from Christ, was born out of his death and resurrection. Had He not died, had He not been resurrected, we would have no hope. We would have no salvation. We would have no reason to hope for a better future beyond this broken world. Had I refused to be completely broken down, He would never have had access to rebuild and restore my life. He broke my world completely open. He began to restore me. He continues to restore me, for His glory, for His purpose, maybe even, for your hope.

I believe that it is no accident you picked up this book. I believe that our heavenly Father, loves you so much that He wants to lead you on paths of righteousness for His name's sake. I believe there is a unique hope that is inside of you right now, as you read these words, a hope that others will need from you. I might be the person who needs you to walk the road you are on. We may never know. But I can tell you this. The world needs you to walk it out with Him. Fight the temptation to run from the pain and into the spiritual grave. Fight the temptation to do this all alone. It may be the hardest work you ever do in your lifetime, but please do it and please oh please, allow someone into this messy process with you. Grab His hand, let Him take you by your right hand, and do the work that must be done. The world needs you. I need you, the unique hope only you can give to this world. There is a cavernous gap in this world filled only when you allow yourself this moment of restoration with Him and step into your personal hope-giving purpose.

Father,

Thank you for this day. Thank you for this moment to come out of the cave and into the light of Your presence. We cannot do this without You. Restore in me, Your heart, Your purpose. Please do not let me continue to walk in the ways that once stole the very spirit from within me. Please be with us as we journey deeper into Your word. Please do not allow me, us, to continue just being readers of Your Word, but hearers and doers. When the journey gets arduous, we look forward to the lush green, life giving, life breathing, green pastures of rest.

Amen

Unveiled

While sitting in church a year of Sundays ago, a heavy revelation washed over me. It was the middle of worship, and honestly, I do not even know what song I was supposed to be singing. I was so completely overcome with emotion as each thought peeled away and revealed the next.

It has bothered me greatly that it has taken me so long to write this book. That I have allowed countless distractions to keep me from doing the work that God has called me to do with this book. But that Sunday morning, I felt a sort of release. As much as I have beaten myself up about it, I could not have finished this book when I first set out to write it.

Let's backtrack a little further.

Years, I mean years and years ago, I felt that the Lord gave me the vision of a women's conference centered around a scripture in 2 Corinthians that talks about beholding the image of God with unveiled faces, even naming the conference in my heart, "Unveiled." A couple of years later, while arguing with my teenage daughter about her countless filters on her pictures, hiding her true beauty, it hit me, the same conference for teen girls would be called "Unfiltered."

Now, back to where I started. That Sunday morning, singing some song I cannot recall, His revelation showed me that I could not have written this book any sooner. I could not have written it any sooner because I was still filtered. I was still *veiled!* In my deep desire to people please, I was filtering my words, both spoken and typed. This entire book would have been written through a filter, not beholding the image of God, but of my own veiled heart.

It has been years more since writing the above few paragraphs, and slowly but surely, I have been prayerfully combing through each word, sentence, and paragraph, allowing the Holy Spirit to remove the veil that I had over my words to you. It has been unbelievably freeing to write without reservation, without filters and veils! Each section, brought before the King, brought in front of the still waters of reflection, each one allowed to rest in the green pastures of scripture, so that His Word, His righteousness might be found for His glory and His purpose in all of our lives. In some areas, I still feel great victory, in others, I see the struggles that have shown themselves more often than I would like to admit.

Why would He unveil me? For you. For me. I love that He showed me that my mouth was covered with silver duct tape. That was my veil. It was hindering me from sharing with you, with myself, who He has shown Himself to be to me. What He has shown me about the twenty-third Psalm. And you know what is most freeing? It is aok with me, for the first time in my entire life, that you might disagree with me. You might see the twenty-third Psalm completely differently. You may see this book as too story laden. You might see it too light on scriptures and too heavy on self-help. And it is ok with me that you see all of that. But I do not see those things. I see these words, each collection of vowels and consonants, as my personal offering of worship to the King who gave each one to me. I offer each back to Him in an act of love and you, my friend, are caught up in the middle of it. My prayer is that it would wash lovingly all over you. That it would envelop you with peace you have never known. Writing this book about Him, for Him, to Him, frees me to rip the tape off and write with an unveiled heart.

In the process of writing this book, I have listened to and learned much from the incredible author, Elizabeth Gilbert. I am absolutely certain that, though we have never met or spoken, she must have written the book, "Big Magic" for me, as a guide, as a mirror to the work I had yet to do inside me. I've read it twice in the last year, each time swelling with hope and belief in my calling to get the Lord's work out of me and into the world, regardless of the outcome, regardless of the way the world receives it. I needed her unique hope to finish this book.

Thank you, Father, for keeping my future path veiled until the time you called me to walk through it. Thank you for being the light to my feet, keeping me from stumbling over my future. Thank you for not allowing me to write a book before unveiling my heart, so that I may behold Your image and not my own! Thank You for the freedom to really write, to really free this word You have given me so many years ago. It is all for You and for Your glory alone. Thank You for every person who has done the hard work ahead of me, offering me their unique hope.

Amen

Even though I walk through the
valley of the shadow of death,
I will fear no evil, for you are with me;
your rod and your staff, they comfort me.

Psalms 23:4

Step by Step

Your word is a lamp to my feet and a light to my path.
Psalm 119:105

It never fails, when my family goes camping, we are never close to the toilets. Odd story starter, I know. At one point, all five of my children were under the age of seven. You are correct. I did say five. I have my own mega family starter kit, and yes, they are all mine. Believe me when I say, that is a lot of little bottoms that have to go potty at two in the morning. And if you have ever raised children, or cared for children of any age, you know, if one asks, they suddenly all have to go. It's like someone figured out how to synchronize bladders like they synchronized Swatch watches in the 80's! It is a miracle I still cannot explain.

In those dark nights, mysteriously every bladder is awake, except for my husband's. It is magical what he can sleep through. These are the times when I have to muster up the courage to leave my tent and use my trusty flashlight to guide my way. I will admit, this big hunk of yellow and black plastic makes for a great flashlight, but as great as it is, it does not reveal the entire the path to the restrooms. That is not what it is created to do, though I so very much wish that it could. This flashlight only lights the steps right in front of me. My children and I must take it step by step on our often-long pilgrimage to the toilets.

Our Great Shepherd is a light for this life, too. He could light the entire way from beginning to end, but He chooses not to. Psalm 119:105 says,

> *"Thy word is a lamp unto my feet, and a light unto my path."*

This light is for our current path, not the miles ahead of us. He promises us that He will light our path, step by step, not block by block, or mile by mile beginning to end. He, in all of His goodness, veils parts of our paths ahead of us.

Could we handle all that He would ask us to endure in life had He revealed it all from the beginning of our journeys?

I cannot fathom the idea of knowing the depth of the pain and heartache that I would have to walk through before I ever had to take the first step. I would undoubtedly measure every last bit of it against my limited human ability to handle it all. It would not take long to assess that I would fail miserably in my own paltry strength. No doubt, I would never be willing to take the first step, or try to manipulate and control everything so as to avoid every last drop of adversity ahead of me. Had I known the battles and pain I would face in the limited time I have been alive; I am not sure I would have chosen to continue living. Even sight unseen, I know I do not have the strength to complete all that is required of me. But His word says in Psalm 73:26,

"My flesh and my heart may fail, but God is the strength of my heart and my portion forever."

I have endured all that I have, only because it was done in His strength and not my own. When I look back on the distance I have traveled, I see His mighty hand and strength at work. I see nothing of my own doing that is worthy of praise. It is all by His hand and for His glory that I am alive and writing to you this morning.

Think back on your life. Think about your battles, your struggles, and the level of strength you had as a child. Had God revealed all that you are recalling, from the very beginning, it would have crushed you emotionally and spiritually. It is too much. He is so loving and so knowing that He measures it out in twenty-four-hour long doses. Even that is broken into day and night. We cannot even carry the weight of an entire day. We need rest. His light is for your feet, for your immediate path. This means there is no need to measure tomorrow's struggles against today's strength. It will not add up. I promise.

I want you to take a moment and really survey the landscape of the life you have lived thus far. Look at the joys, the struggles, the mundane, the magnificent, all of it. Do not look forward, just look back. Do you ever stop and wonder how in the world you even survived it all? I do not know about the roads you have walked, but when I personally look back, I am overwhelmed. I think to myself, with gut honesty, I could never do that again, and Lord, I pray, I never have to do it again! But, with His help and strength, here I am today, on the other side of some seemingly insurmountable mountains. I stop and I give tremendous thanks, that those days are already over and that I never had to walk out my days knowing what was to come.

I do not know what tomorrow holds, either. His light is shining on this minute, as I write to you now. His light is here, in this moment with me. As much as I hate to admit the amount of work I am still doing on my uncanny ability to worry about the future, I don't really want to know the truth of all that it contains. I do not have what it takes to walk it out yet. I am building that today. This kind of puts worry into perspective for me. Worry about an unseen time and place and situation is fiction. The presence and strength from my Shepherd, that will enable me to endure any of it, is real. Regardless of what lies ahead, I know Who will be with me when I get there.

Father,

Thank You for one day at a time, one step at a time. Thank You for knowing better than I, what I need to know. Thank You for battling wars I will never know You fought. Oh, that You pulled back the veil and I could see just all that You, in Your unlimited strength, do on my behalf.

I love You so!

Amen

Deep Darkness

In the translation that I read from, the English Standard Version, the phrase "Valley of death" is also noted as the "Valley of deep darkness." This is a place where I have taken up residency, much of my adult life. I have shared quite a bit about the painful past that I have walked through, and to be honest, much of it was walked without seeking God in any capacity. I felt that I was often walking alone in my struggles with nothing more than a big, yellow, and black flashlight.

The footnote at the bottom of my ESV study Bible talks about the deserts of Judah. It details that there in these deserts, it so dark that one would not know if there were any predators lurking nearby, be it human attackers, or ravenous animal. This is the epitome of deep darkness. I cannot begin to imagine traveling this way. I highly doubt that at the time this was written, anyone had a battery or solar operated flashlight.

This verse reaffirms a desperate need for deep dependence on our Father in the midst of the deepest of dark times. These are the times when you are not sure what problem is lurking nearby, when the other shoe is surely going to drop. These uncertain times, shrouded in darkness, are unnerving at best.

Verse four also reminds us that even though we are walking through this deep darkness, this valley of death, we do not have to fear evil, for His rod and staff are there to comfort us. Take a look that those words again. "You are with me. Your rod and your staff, they comfort me."

He is with us. He did not pack us a sack lunch and hand off His rod and staff for the voyage ahead. He is with us. He is the one carrying the rod and the staff. How cool is that thought? We are in the midst of deep darkness, and He is there, too!

Thinking back to the footnote at the bottom of my Bible, where it discusses the idea that the desert was a place of unfathomable darkness, we can view the rod and staff through a different lens. In such a setting, in a time before guns and other modern weapons of defense, these items could have very well been used to defend and protect their possessors. When we read this verse against the backdrop of defense, we can see that our Heavenly Father is also our great defender and protector.

What great comfort His rod and staff bring when we see them as weapons fashioned to keep us safe in the midst of the darkest times in our lives; the moments when we cannot see our hands right in front of our spiritual faces. In those moments we may not see Him, but we know that He is not only with us, He is wielding weapons formed to protect and defend us from all that is unseen and unknown.

The apostle Paul describes these weapons in his second letter to the Corinthians,
"For the weapons of our warfare are not of the flesh but have divine power to destroy strongholds."
2 Corinthians 10:4

He understood very well that we are not waging war in flesh alone, but also in very spiritual realms.

What a beautiful and comforting thought, our Shepherd is walking alongside us, in the darkest season, wielding the perfect weapons, to keep us from the attacks of both the physical and the spiritual, that try constantly to assail us.

Along with the safety benefit that a rod and a staff would bring, there is yet another view on these two treasures.

I am not sure about you, but I grew up in a generation that threw around the phrase, "Spare the rod, spoil the child." Side note, this is not a scripture, but an interpretation of one in Proverbs. Nonetheless, I heard this often, leading me to see the word "rod" and always see it as a discipline measure. Discipline measures never seem to equate to a comforting measure to a child, and having been both parent and child, I can say with confidence, they do not bring much comfort to a parent either.

But, what if maybe they are? Parenting gurus will tell you that children respond best to parents who are clear and consistent with boundaries, expectations, and discipline. As a former teacher, I will share with you that I have experienced children who come from these secure and consistent backgrounds, and they seem to be more emotionally stabile, great problem solvers, and best of all- they are more resilient.

So, maybe, His rod and staff are there to create clear and consistent boundaries, expectations, and maybe even discipline. Maybe they are there because He is the ultimate Father who loves me, loves you. In those seasons of deep darkness, it seemed unfair to have to deal with discipline for my husband's actions as well as my own.

If then the rod and the staff are also a form of discipline, we can see them as the loving act of a heavenly Father. In Deuteronomy we see several references to a biblical view of discipline.

"Know then in your heart that, as a man disciplines his son, the Lord your God disciplines you." 8:5

"And consider today (since I am not speaking to your children who have not known or seen it), consider the discipline of the Lord your God, his greatness, his mighty hand, and his outstretched arm," 11:2

Job even references God's discipline:

"Behold, blessed is the one whom God reproves; therefore, despise not the discipline of the Almighty"
Job 5:17

Many times in scripture we see reference to God's love for us through His discipline and correction of us.

I will be the first to admit, my life sometimes seemed to be a never-ending barrage of hard times. It was so hard to see my Shepherd with me in those dark times. Truth be told, it is hard to see anything in the dark at all. But He was there. I was never alone. I was always enveloped in His love.

It is easy to believe that God has left our side when we cannot "see" Him. When we cannot "sense" Him near to us, we feel all alone. When the world seems so dark, our skewed reality tells us that if we cannot see Him, sense Him, touch Him, He must not be there. But it just isn't so.

Luke 1:79 speaks of Jesus:

"to give light to those who sit in darkness and in the shadow of death, to guide our feet into the way of peace."

Jesus, Son of God, is my Shepherd. He longs to be my light in my deepest darkness. To be my guide, with rod and staff, the light unto my uncertain path. What great comfort to know that He is with us, even when we cannot see Him. What peace to know that His discipline of me is an assertion of His perfect love for me.

Where do you stand on this? How do you feel about the idea of the rod and staff being a tool, a weapon, forged to protect you in those times when you feel all alone in deep darkness? Does it comfort you? Does it even seem real? Can you look back at your dark times and see that protection over your life?

What about the rod and staff being a tool for discipline? I can only fathom that for some, discipline was done incorrectly at home, as a child, and the idea of the rod and the staff being discipline is not one of comfort. If this is the case, and someone abused you as a child, I pray you will reach out to someone for help and healing. This kind of discipline is not godly. Godly discipline, while not fun in any measure, is not harmful to your flesh or your spirit. It is done in love, never anger or hate. Please know that our Father would never abuse you. I beg of you, if you have not reached out for help and healing for past abuse, please let this be the gentle nudge to do so now.

The last question I feel led to ask; do you see Him when you look back? Scripture says He is right there with us. Do you see His fingerprints anywhere?

I remember when our youngest was seven or eight, she wanted to learn to float. One night she finally surrendered her nerves, laid on her back and allowed her daddy to help her balance on the top of the water. As he held her lightly, her little body breathing in and out, he stood between her and the stairs entering the pool. As children came into the pool splashing, he deflected their splashes from hitting her body. He knew that one splash would be enough to startle her and keep her from learning how to float. She never knew he did this. But, as I watched him hold her there, deflecting water from hitting her unknowing little body, I had to assume our heavenly Father has very much done the same thing in our lives.

Though the deep darkness veils His activity around me, I trust that He is acting on my behalf. That He is standing between me and unknown forces, shielding me and allowing me to surrender to the work I must learn to do. He is a good, good Father.

I feel that I must share this with you. Going back to the scripture in Psalm 119, and the song many of us memorized in the eighties, *"Thy word is a lamp unto my feet and a light unto my path."* Knowing the context of that time, knowing that there were no street lights, knowing it was pitch black outside after the sun had set, makes this verse critical. But, what I want you to really notice is the first five words in the verse, 'thy word is a lamp.' Friend, if all I have to light the blinding darkness around me is the word of God, and I don't know the word of God, I am in trouble. I have no light at all. This isn't me preaching at you, or even me. This is a reality check. Without the word of God, opened and poured into our hearts and spirits, all we do have is a big, chunky, yellow and black flashlight without any batteries. And the world is still literally and figuratively impenetrably dark. And we cannot see all of the dangers that surely surround us.

Oh Father,

I do not know how to receive Your discipline, most of the time. Honestly, it often feels more like attack than redirection, or even direction. It is so hard to frame Your loving guidance as loving sometimes. Please help me to open my eyes to see Your truth, Your word and to receive it as Yours, even when it doesn't feel good to the flesh or spirit. Thank You for loving me and adopting me as Your own daughter. Thank You for loving me enough to choose the refining of discipline to shape and mold me to be more and more reflecting of Your glory, not my own.

I love You so!

Amen

Anchored

July 29th

"COME TO ME CONTINUALLY. I am meant to be the Center of your consciousness, the *Anchor of your soul*." Young, Sarah. *Jesus Calling: devotions for every day of the year*. Liturgical, 2008. Print.

Anchored.

What a powerful word to describe our relationship to God, like Him or not. It is the reason believers feel secure and the reason many choose not to believe in Him at all. July 29th's Jesus Calling entry really got my mind going. I am a huge believer in journaling, so I felt led to share my journal entry with you from that date.

"I love that we have created a short tether together. In many seasons of my life, I did not turn to you. I barely knew you. **But you were my anchor all along.** With the long tether between us, I rarely felt your tug, unless I drifted really far away. Sometimes, the rope was so long, it did not seem my boat was tied to an anchor at all. **But there you were, in the same place all along.** It was me who drifted away from you.

Even though it seemed you had moved from me, that is not the nature of an anchor. An anchor stays in one spot. When it felt like I had not heard from you, or felt your tug on my heart, it was only because the rope was so long between us that it took that long for me to feel you resisting against my far stretching drift. But then I would feel you and I would begin to return to the center. As I returned, the same waves of doubt, fear, and temptation would toss me and send me away from you. **But you were always in the same spot, never moving.**

The more I have gotten to know you, the harder I have worked with you to shorten the rope. I feel your tugs often. We get so close in distance, sometimes, it seems that the waves can't/don't have the space to come between us. When I *have allowed space between us, that is when I make room for storms to come between us.*

But there you are. You never moved. You keep me centered. You never leave me. You are always in the same place, anchored in my heart."

What a great eye-opener the anchor was for me. My tether was long, so long I had no idea it was even tethered to Him at all. The length of the tether is not as important as is who I was tethered to. I was tethered to my Source, my Anchor. He has never moved. He has always been there. How often do we feel like He has left us?

I remember when my marriage was in the pits of hell, I felt truly alone. My husband was living his own life, my children were young, and I had run off most friends and family because I would not sever my marriage when they thought I should have. I remember sitting in our tv room, sitting on our bed, sitting in my car, knowing I needed God, but felt hopelessly far from His reach, let alone His presence. I had no idea that He was there with me, on the couch, on my bed, in my car, holding my shattered pieces in His loving hands.

He was always there, even when my feeble fingers could not trace His presence, nor my heart hear the beating of His. He was at work in my life, ever present, well proved.

Our Shepherd, our Anchor is immovable, unshakeable. He is right there, right where we left Him. He is with us in the deep darkness of the valleys. He is with us in the bright light of day on the mountain tops. He is with us. Even when our senses fail to detect Him. That is our human failure, not His absence.

My friend, He is with you even now. I know you may not see Him, but that does not make Him absent. Are the storms raging between you and your belief? Maybe the tether is short, and you feel Him calling to you often, and He feels closer to you than your own heart beating in your chest. Either way, He is where He said He would be. He is with you always.

"And behold, I am with you always, to the end of the age." Matthew 28:20

This promise, from Jesus to His disciples, is our hope today. The very same Jesus is with us from the beginning of time to the end of the age, the end of time. With us. Present. Emmanuel. God with us.

Father,

Thank You for being our anchor, well proved, ever present. Thank You for being our Emmanuel. Thank You for never leaving our side, even when our unbelief tells us that You are long gone, that Your grace for us has run out. Thank You that I do not have to see You to know You are here. Please forgive my doubting heart, my unbelieving senses. Help me to see Your presence all around me. I love You so!

Amen

Front Porch of the Soul

This morning, I was recalling a special visual a friend gave to me some years ago when I was in one of the darkest valley seasons of my life. She said that God wanted to hold me, like sit in His lap like a child. I wanted nothing more, but I felt so far from God, I did not know if I could ever find my way to His loving embrace.

As I journaled, the many instances of His loving nearness and presence flooded my memories. Memories from the very same season in which I felt furthest from God and most alone in my life.

He was not only there with me, my well proved Anchor, He was active in my life. He was the discernment I desperately needed in a sea of a thousand voices. When my life shattered into such small fragments they could not be pieced together by human hands, He was the dust taker and life re-maker. He was there with me, stretching every quarter and nickel in the gas tank. He was there with me, in the grocery store, making every last dollar bill spend further. He was, and continues to be, the shield that guards my mind from memories that no longer serve a purpose to me or others.

What I saw this morning was His loving presence that had been holding me, rocking me, just like I desperately needed, on the front porch of my soul. Even when my circumstances clouded my awareness of Him, I was always in His loving embrace.

His word promises that He is always with us. Time and time again we see Scriptures that tell of His nearness. But sometimes, specifically in the hard times, it is incredibly hard to discern His presence, but rest assured my dear friend, He is fully present.

One day, when the clouds of pain roll back, and the skies of your memories are clear, you will see His fingerprints everywhere. You will look back and you too, will see Him holding you, rocking you, on the front porch of your soul.

Father,

I cannot thank You enough for holding me, for enveloping me in Your presence. I thought I was alone, when all I wanted was for You to hold me tight, to keep me safe. And You did. Please forgive my unseeing eye. Please forgive my doubting heart. You were there, always. Please help us to continue to see Your fingerprints all around us, even today. I love You so!

Amen

Right-Handed God

"Nevertheless, I am continually with you; you hold my right hand." Psalms 73:23

As I reread the scripture above, I cannot help but note that the Psalmist makes mention of the Lord holding him by his right hand. This statement is following the words that acknowledge the very fact that he is with God continually. By saying that his hand is being held by the Creator of the Universe, he is pointing to the very nearness and intimacy of God.

I want you to stop for a moment and think about the act of having your hand held. What, or better yet who, comes to mind? Why did that person, or those people, come to mind for you? I believe that hand holding is not only intimate, it is in this case, the act of God's leadership.

Will you go with me for a memory jogger? When my littles were actually little, holding a hand was an act of safety. I did this to keep them near to me and to keep them from harm. Had they been allowed to be free range chickens with their little heads cut off, well you and I both know what could have been their fate. When we frame this scripture within the context of the twenty-third Psalm, we see God doing the same thing in the midst of the Valley of the Shadow of Death.

This all circles right back around to the rod and staff we previously talked about. We talked about His rod and staff being a source of safety and protection. It seems to me, His nearness, His hand holding, is the very same thing, a source of safety and protection. He knows that if we were let loose, free range chickens with our heads cut off, what our eternal fate would be.

Now, before you go on a rabbit trail in the wrong direction, please allow me to clarify. I do not believe that God usurps our free will, only to impose His own. It does not take long to observe that we humans are all over the place with our choices, both good and not so good. I believe this is why He, knowing our humanness, sent the spotless lamb, His son Jesus, to be the living sacrifice our human nature would require.

In the midst of all of our choices, He gave us His word to learn from and be led by, almost as if by holding it in our grasp, we are holding His hand. I have heard it said several times that the Bible is the only book that can read you. His word is within us, that is, if we will allow it the soul penetration it requires.

Can I ask you a question? What is your quiet time like in this season? You know, your time set aside to pray, sing, learn the word of God, journal, etc., what is it like right now? Are you in a season of regular time of devotion to His word? Are you in a season, devoid of time at all, because life has more demands than twenty-four hours can cover? Are you somewhere in the middle?

Yeah, me too.

I am definitely more in the middle right now. I try to beat the rooster; I mean the third alarm's fourth snooze button. I set the coffee pot to wake itself up and get to work, making me some go juice at some ungodly hour. All of this to motivate me to get into the Word before the world wakes up and starts trying to demand of me, define me, trying to put its word in me. And some days I am great at getting up at "Oh Lord Thirty" as my mother calls it. And some days, there are not enough alarms to convince me that the Bible is more inviting than my warm cocoon of a bed.

But when I do. When I crawl out of bed, pour myself a cup of joe, crawl under a blanket on the couch and pullout my Bible and books, oh the goodness that follows! I cannot express the power of starting my day in the Word of God. There is this indescribable moment when reading scriptures and I read the same one for the four hundredth time and I see it like I have never seen it before. And the freedom that follows. The instruction I receive that finally sinks in. This all goes back to getting my fill at the well of Living Water. The whole tone of the day is drastically different.

Let me be super clear, I am not saying that having quiet time has some magical powers that prevent struggle and trials. I am simply saying that the investment of time fills me to the full with the Word, not leaving space for filling from the world.

There is a difference from when I spend real time reading, studying, and journaling, and the days when I simply do all of the above to check a box off and start the day. Those check box days are the days that my actions scream allegiance to routine, not whisper gentle devotion to the King, my Shepherd. Pretending is pretending. Checking a box is only a boxed checked. But sometimes, what starts as simply a routine turns into something simply out of this world. The Creator of all, meets me in my routine and rocks my world upside down and uses the mundane to show me something so much more.

This quiet time, drawing closer to the Word of God, saddles me right up to His right side. The very thought makes me think of my Popi, my mother's father. I can smell his aftershave and feel the warmth of his embrace. I always loved drawing near to him, snuggling into his armpit, wrapped in his arms.

Can it be that my quiet time affords me the same opportunity, to draw near to Him, snuggle up to His right side, wrapped in His loving embrace? I think so. I have felt His word come to life, felt the pain, the urgency, the love that covered the pages. The intentionality that Moses shared with his people, as he told them he would not be with them as they made it to the Promised Land. It broke my heart. I could sense everyone's emotion as I read it. I sensed Him as near as my Popi's warm breath on my head.

If you are in a season that keeps you from this precious time, do not let legalism bind you up in guilt. Our heavenly Father is a gentleman, and He will meet you right where you are. Seek Him while you drive to work.

Talk to Him while you grocery shop. Let Him sing over you while you sing the baby back to sleep for the third time tonight. And if you are able, sneak in a moment to crack open His word. Allow it to wash over you. It may be more refreshing than the shower you haven't had the time to take since the baby was born, three years ago. Take off the shackles of legalism. Seek His face as only you are able to in this season.

Father,

I lift up my friend to You. Not every season is easy to set aside time to be with You and I thank You for the grace You offer. I thank You that we can come to You anytime and anywhere! I praise You that You are not hidden from me, hidden behind a veil, in the Holy of Holies. You are accessible and I pray that we would all make You a priority, that you would meet us all there in our efforts to know You better.

I love You so!

Amen

Even Though

When I read the words of the fourth verse of the twenty-third Psalm, my heart skips an unwelcomed beat at the onset. Those two words "even though" are quite possibly some of the most difficult words to stomach. "Even though" simply put, means that regardless, despite, still. It implies that something is going on that requires perseverance and continuing on.

The author and prophet, Habakkuk stated these same two words in the midst of great tribulation:

"Even though the fig trees have no blossoms, and there are no grapes on the vines; even though the olive crop fails, and the fields lie empty and barren; even though the flocks die in the fields, and the cattle barns are empty, yet I will rejoice in the Lord! I will be joyful in the God of my salvation! The Sovereign Lord is my strength! He makes me as surefooted as a deer, able to tread upon the heights. Habakkuk 3:17-19 NLT

Even though everything about what Habakkuk could see was utter destruction, and no good could be tangibly found, he declared his faith and dedication to God.

Even though.

The Psalmist, King David, did the same in verse four.

"Even though I walk through the valley of the shadow of death, I will fear no evil, for you are with me; your rod and your staff, they comfort me."

David is talking about this deep darkness, the desert valley, a place where he cannot see his hand before his face, and even though he is in this place none of us would want to be, he affirms his faith and comfort found in God, his perfect Shepherd.

A thought struck me this morning, as I read the words of the twenty-third Psalm, for what must have been the three hundred millionth time. David is speaking from real life experience. He has been the shepherd and he has been the king. In this Psalm, he makes himself to be the other party. In more than half of this Psalm, he is the sheep. He knows from the shepherd's point of view, just what a sheep needs to survive, and he embodies the role from that point of view, making his heavenly Father, his good Shepherd. Then, to close the scripture, he takes on the role as honored guest, placing God as his heavenly Host and King.

Many, many times, Jesus tells us that He is the Good Shepherd, that we can only enter the heavenly gates through Him. As we talked about before, He asserts that we know His voice and will follow Him. We also read in Revelation and 1 Timothy, that Jesus is our King of Kings, Lord of Lords.

David knows his reality. He does not sweep it under the rug. He does not try to sugar coat it or cover it in a million filters to post it on social media. He is in the valley of the shadow of death and he acknowledges it.

Even though. Two words that acknowledge the pain, names the trials, sheds light on darkness. Still, they are also two words that though they acknowledge the current circumstance, also acknowledge the belief, the perseverance, the power to press on, for he knows Who is with him, and he is comforted. Even though.

And as it turns out, "even though" offers hope. It drives a stake in the ground, raises a flag of victory, and shouts that in the midst of the trial, my strength, my faith, my belief, my hope comes from the Lord, the maker of Heaven and Earth! Even though my circumstances look slightly less than dire, I see life, I see what is yet to come! Even though speaks life to the life that has yet to be revealed, rather than the visible, tangible world before us.

Have you ever been there? Do you know what I mean by dreading those words, "even though"? Have you walked through so many trials and struggles that the thought of one more "even though" scenario is more than you can stomach? Maybe you are there now? Does the thought of "even though" offer you a spark of hope? Will you pray with me?

Father,

Thank you for always being with me, even when I cannot sense you at all. Thank you for being the strength I have desperately needed to persevere, and the well-proved comfort in my trials. You are with me. You protect me. I have never liked the idea of having to preface my belief in you with, "even though", because it acknowledges I am going through something. I am so sorry. Please forgive my selfishness. I hate pain. I hate hurting, emotionally, physically. Even though I am walking through this season of struggle, I know that you are with me. Your word and your presence, they comfort me. I love you, so!

Amen

You prepare a table before me
in the presence of my enemies;
you anoint my head with oil;
my cup overflows.

Psalms 23:5

Our Shepherd, Our Father

I feel the need to start this chapter by discussing another famous Biblical father, the father of the Prodigal Son. This was a wise and fair man who had chosen to give both of his sons an inheritance. At the strong request of his second and more immature, impulsive son, his portion of the inheritance early, without any stipulations or strings.

As any reasonable, logical parent would expect, the thoughtless son quickly squandered it away. All too quickly, his world fell apart all around him. It did not take awfully long for him to realize his grave error. I have to believe that while in his season of absolute destitution, he found himself in the deepest valley of darkness. Let us take a closer look at how it all went down in Luke 15.

"And he (Jesus) said, "There was a man who had two sons. And the younger of them said to his father, 'Father, give me the share of property that is coming to me.' And he divided his property between them. Not many days later, the younger son gathered all he had

and took a journey into a far country, and there he squandered his property in reckless living. And when he had spent everything, a severe famine arose in that country, and he began to be in need. So, he went and hired himself out to one of the citizens of that country, who sent him into his fields to feed pigs. And he was longing to be fed with the pods that the pigs ate, and no one gave him anything."

"But when he came to himself, he said, 'How many of my father's hired servants have more than enough bread, but I perish here with hunger! I will arise and go to my father, and I will say to him, "Father, I have sinned against heaven and before you. I am no longer worthy to be called your son. Treat me as one of your hired servants." (v. 11-19)

"*But when he came to himself*" When this young man realized the gravity of his choices, when he had been led beside the still waters of self-reflection, in that place of deep darkness, he realized that even those who work for his father had all of their needs met and decided he should return home to be like one of the hired servants. He had to find himself in the bottom of a pig trough, his greatest pit, to be led by still waters.

I have been there. I have had the desires to do it by myself. Man, I sound like a three-year-old when I type that. Time and time again I have found myself in the same place as the impulsive son, needing to control my own outcomes, needing my heavenly Father to give me what He has planned for me in my own timing. And every single time, I have caused more harm than good for myself. Taking control, or should I say, trying to take control out of His hands, has always left me feeling more out of control than when I first let my impulses take the lead. But in the midst of my pit, when I felt I couldn't sink any deeper, I found this stillness, and the Lord allowed me to come to the end myself.

I love what happens next in this story. Maybe I should be more honest, I need what happens next in this story.

The son returns home to his father, completely humbled and broken, prepared for the well-deserved rejection and shame awaiting him. He is a lost sheep who has run off far from his flock, and now is returning to his shepherd, his father, when something unexpected, better yet, something undeserved happens.

'And he arose and came to his father. But while he was still a long way off, his father saw him and felt compassion, and ran and embraced him and kissed him.
(v. 20)

The scriptures tell us that his father sees him coming from a long way off. A long way off. Do you see it? Read it again! "*But while he was still a long way off, his father saw him*".

His father was *looking* for him!

He was expectantly hopeful for him! This child he had surely asked the local prayer team to be praying for. This child whom he lost endless nights' sleep over, wondering if he had made the worst parenting choices ever. This child who he wondered if he would ever have a chance at reconciliation with. This was the child he did not know if he would ever hold in his arms again. He was looking for him! And then he saw him, the son he was looking for, scanning the horizon for, praying for, agonizingly waiting for, and he felt compassion for him and ran to embrace him. There was no shame or guilt trips. There was no rejection. There was only a father's unconditional love.

And the son said to him, 'Father, I have sinned against heaven and before you. I am no longer worthy to be called your son.' (v. 21)

The son, like so many of us, starts rattle-trapping about all of his mistakes, hoping, at best, to earn his father's grace. He knows how gravely he has sinned against his father and family. He knows he has screwed up and he is prepared for the worst. He has braced for impact. He has braced for the human rejection he knows he is due. But what he gets instead is far more powerful, more impactful in this young man's life.

But the father said to his servants, 'Bring quickly the best robe, and put it on him, and put a ring on his hand, and shoes on his feet. And bring the fattened calf and kill it and let us eat and celebrate. For this my son was dead, and is alive again; he was lost, and is found.' And they began to celebrate." (v22-24)

The father tells his servants to prepare a feast in his son's honor. He tells them to run and get a robe and a ring and even sandals for his feet. A robe and shoes. Think about that. What condition can you imagine his clothing and shoes were in? He had been working in a pig's trough, barely surviving. He had been walking for who knows how long, how many days, how many miles.

His shoes, if he had any on, would have surely been worn out. His father gave him clean clothes and shoes. And the ring. I have read it elsewhere that this ring was the family ring. Even had it been just a ring, this lavish gift was an extra, unexpected gift, that one who hoped only for grace could never have seen coming.

This gracious father also sends for the fattened calf to be slaughtered. Why? This is a choice meat selection. Fit for a feast, a party, for the son who has returned after much prayer on the father's part. He chose the fattened calf for his malnourished son.

This lavish, unexpected outpouring of love from the father is a brutal slap across the face of the first-born child, the wiser, more calculated and planned out, older brother. A brother who was faithful to his father and the gifts he had been given. This flies all over him and sends him into a jealous rage.

"Now his older son was in the field, and as he came and drew near to the house, he heard music and dancing. And he called one of the servants and asked what these things meant. And he said to him, 'Your brother has come, and your father has killed the fattened calf, because he has received him back safe and sound.' But he was angry and refused to go in. His father came out and entreated him, but he answered his father, 'Look, these many years I have served you, and I never disobeyed your command, yet you never gave me a young goat, that I might celebrate with my friends. But when this son of yours came, who has devoured your property with prostitutes, you killed the fattened calf for him!' And he said to him, 'Son, you are always with me, and all that is mine is yours. It was fitting to celebrate and be glad, for this your brother was dead, and is alive; he was lost, and is found.'" (v. 25-32)

Do you see yourself in this story? Unfortunately, I do. I can see myself as the older brother, more often than I would care to admit. I am a rule follower/peace maker who is constantly trying to do all of the right things, thus why my testimony isn't more full of spicy, relatable details. I am the one who tries to do all that I can, to obey as much as I can. I do not ever want anyone to be mad at me. So, I become the older brother, incensed that the younger, squandering brother, gets away with a sin filled life and gets the same celebration and grace as I do! But God! Didn't you see me trying to do all that You commanded of me? Did you not see that I was where I was supposed to be, doing what You have called me to be doing? Didn't You see me trying to earn Your grace and celebration?

What?!

That is as ugly coming out of my mouth as it is living in my heart! Ugly as it is, it has taken up residency for far too many years of my life. So many opportunities to celebrate others who have found their faith, returned to His undeserved grace. But instead, I have chosen not to go in, not to attend the party, not to eat of the fattened calf because my heart is already fattened with jealousy and bitterness.

And then I see it. My life as the older, bitter brother has left me in a pit of jealousy, feeding with the pigs, a long way off from my Father. I too, broken, spent, and far from home, long to return to the One who is still watching for me.

Cue the beautiful soundtrack. While you and I were a long way off, while we were in the pig troughs and deep dark pits of life, our Heavenly Father was scanning the horizon for us. He was looking for you, for me, in the distance. Can you see our heavenly Father in this? Can you see Him scanning the horizon for your return? Can you see Him pacing the front porch of His heavenly dwelling, waiting for your return and then, upon seeing you, He runs to you, to hold you, embrace you, kiss you? And then, He covers you with a robe of righteousness and adorns you with a ring! Scripture reminds us of His lavish loving response:

"But now thus says the Lord, he who created you, O Jacob, he who formed you, O Israel: "Fear not, for I have redeemed you; I have called you by name, you are mine. When you pass through the waters, I will be with you; and through the rivers, they shall not overwhelm

you; when you walk through fire you shall not be burned, and the flame shall not consume you. For I am the Lord your God, the Holy One of Israel, your Savior. I give Egypt as your ransom, Cush and Seba in exchange for you. Because you are precious in my eyes, and honored, and I love you, I give men in return for you, peoples in exchange for your life.
Isaiah 43:1-4

Oh, I pray you didn't miss it. *"and I love you."* The very creator of the universe just declared that He loves you. Wow! You, I, we are the disciples who Jesus loves.

Father,

Thank you for always scanning the horizon for me. Thank you for searching for my return. Thank you for never giving up on me. Please forgive my doubting of you, and my jealousy of others. Thank you for loving me when I was the younger son, and when I was the older. I love you, too!

Amen

My Redeemer

So, when I say that I am a recovering people pleaser, I am not kidding. My twisted-up guts would love if I were kidding. The very thought of sitting down at a table, prepared by God, with me at the head and all the honored guests seated at the table being my enemies, talk about awkward! I am not one who likes to stick out. I would much prefer to blend in. This makes me an excellent choir member. No solos for this chick!

Part of what kept me from finishing the writing of this book, for literally a decade, is the fear of being rejected by others. I worried and stressed about what people would think about what I had to say. I did not want what I had to say to alienate me from anyone, knowing full well that it could. I did not want my writing to make me stand out from the crowd.

While I would not say that I have any enemies, I would say that I have many people who know me well, and even those who love me, as well as people who do not know me at all, who disagree with many things I say and write. I have been criticized and scrutinized by those who do not share my beliefs, but even more so, by those who share my belief system.

It has been a debilitating thought to put myself, my thoughts out into the open, knowing all of the above could very well happen, leaving but a remnant of close friends and loved ones. I know we are not created to worship what they think and/or have their approval, but if you go back to the beginning of this section, you will be quickly reminded, I am a recovering people pleaser. Still, there is something special about knowing that my Creator would redeem me in the face of them all.

It is interesting to me the way that the Psalmist illustrates this scene unfolding, and beholding redemption, in the presence of his adversaries. Just like the prodigal son was warmly welcomed with celebratory preparations, in the face of his resentful brother, so our Heavenly Father prepares a welcoming feast, a feast of redemption, even in the presence of the disdain-filled faces of those who do not love, support, and may even oppose you.

One afternoon after work, I was standing outside with one of my friends. She was wrestling with the next steps in her career. What worried her most was the future of her children. If she made one career move, it meant relocating her children. If she remained where she was, her little ones would be sacrificing in other areas.

And that is when it hit me. As parents, we can never screw up so big that God is not bigger still to fix it. That is a pretty big statement to digest. Take a moment. Sit with that idea for a moment. Do not rush over this one. As parents, we always seem to think that we can somehow, in our human ability, out do God's ability to cover and, or even redeem us. But the truth is, we just are not that powerful. In fact, we are nowhere near capable of derailing what God has set into motion.

My childhood was the best my parents could give me, and yet there was pain and heartache. I tried to give my children the best childhood I knew how to give, and they all still have heartache and pain. I worried for much of my early marriage that all the turmoil we endured would damage my children for a lifetime.

But, in that moment, with my friend, it all came into focus. Just like I have had countless friendships, guides, and mentors, as well as seemingly random encounters that have changed the trajectory of my life, so will my children and my friend's children, too. Psalm 50:10 reminds us that God owns the *cattle on a thousand hills*. If He has that, then I feel confident that He also has the resources and the armies of angels that will surely be needed to help my children heal from all the hardships they have already and will walk through.

He redeems me. He redeems you, too. You are not in this alone. He is walking through the valley of the shadow of death with you. He is going to guide you along still waters of reflection and protect you with His rod and staff. And then, after coming out of that incredibly dark time, He is going to prepare a table of celebration for you, in the presence of all who doubted you would ever overcome, get clean, get out of debt, get your marriage back in shape, get healthy. Right there, in front of them all, He will redeem you.

I have certainly learned that this celebration in the 23rd Psalm is not a party full of accolade-filled attendees. My redemption, your redemption, is not about their approval, but rather our victory. I am going to need us both to slow down and to read that again. *My redemption, your redemption, is not about their approval, but rather our victory.* This journey of restoration and redemption is about our victory in Him. It has never been about their eventual approval of us, though you would think much of my life's work declared it was.

The footnote for this verse, found in my ESV study Bible, denotes the idea that the enemies mentioned are powerless to stop the celebration and even goes on to note that they are held captive at a victory celebration.

I am not sure I love the idea of people being held captive, against their will, and forced to watch the Lord's redemption of me. But, when I sit with the idea, I realize that at times, we are all held captive by the celebrations of others, even those who we do not care for. We are held captive by sheer curiosity at how they achieved something we have yet to achieve. We are powerless to stop looking on, as we wonder how they gained ground in an area of life that we have so much ground yet to gain. We look on, wondering why not us? Though we may not be their enemies, or adversaries, could it be said that some of these people are people we are not too fond of?

It is all fun and exciting to think of God, keeping out a watchful eye, scanning the deep distance for us, then running to greet us and adorn us with great things beyond what we deserve.

It is an entirely different thing to think of others who have betrayed us, receiving the same favor and adoration. We find ourselves seated on the other side of the prepared table, looking on as God's chosen one is seated in the seat of highest honor, the seat of redemption.

This person has taken the journey from submission, to restoration, and now to the moment of redemption, and we are held captive by our thoughts of "Why not us?". In that moment, we are, I am, the bigger brother, angry with my Heavenly Father, that He would bestow such grace on that person who hurt me so deeply, after I had been so faithful for so long. I am the older brother who kept legalistic score and then threw it back in God's face, regardless of the grace that has overwhelmed me for years. Regardless of the fact that I have been given the luxury of being with Him all along.

We can all be redeemed. It is why Christ came, ministered, died, and rose from the dead. He did all that

He did so that we could be redeemed, while we were still unredeemable. Romans 5:8 says:

"but God shows his love for us in that while we were still sinners, Christ died for us."

While we were careless, immature prodigal sons, scandalously squandering away His lavish gift of grace, He gave His life for us. While we were still acting like jealous, grudge-holding, score keeping big brothers, He gave His life for us.

"For God so loved the world, that he gave his only Son, that whoever believes in him should not perish but have eternal life." John 3:16

Because He wanted an eternity with you, me, every person who has ever hurt us, or even abandoned us, He sent Christ to Earth to suffer at the hands of His accusers and abusers, so that we all would have a chance to sit in the place of the highest honor, a place we could never earn the right to be, the redemption seat, even giving Himself as the fattened calf, slaughtered and sacrificed, in celebration of our return.

Thank You, Father, for preparing a place for us. A place of redemption. A table setting for everyone. A place of grace for all of us. Thank You for being an example for all of us and a reminder that we all need all of You. Thank you for being the watchful Father and the undeserved, perfect Sacrifice.

I love you so!

Amen

Invisible Enemies

It was not very long ago that I had a major breakthrough while I was riding in the car with my husband. As we were talking, I asked him for some advice. See, I was really struggling with a lot of anxiety that day. It was one of those gloomy days where the skies are just filled with low hanging, gray clouds and the spirit feels just as overcast as the sky looks.

I was curious what Scott, who being the person who knows me best, thought my issue was. And like usual, he was spot on. I was going back to my old patterns of people pleasing and that day I was letting it completely consume me and inevitably wreck me.

In my mind, I started going back over the things plaguing me that day. First, I was worried about offending a client with my answer to his request, and so I did not put up boundaries that I needed to put up. Then, I was worried that I had offended a friend of mine because I could not follow through with something, I had impulsively thought that I could do, yet never prayed over. Lastly, I was worried I had upset yet another friend, because I had not gotten to the place where I needed to be, in the time frame I assumed he needed me to be there.

The thing about each of these situations is that every, last one of them were imagined. I should clarify, the situations that caused me angst were real, but each person's reaction to them were not real. There was not a shred of evidence that any of these people were actually upset with me. As I shared all of these worries with my husband, one aha moment after another washed over me.

As he helped me to process through all these thoughts and worries, the emotional floor fell out from under me. I never had any imaginary friends growing up. I only had imaginary enemies.

I spent my whole life worrying about what people thought of me. I spent the whole of my existence working my tail end off, trying not to offend anyone and trying not to make others have any reason to not like me, all the while believing that many of them did not like me no matter how hard I strived to be perfect.

In all the work that I have done to try to figure out the root cause of my people pleasing, I have dug down and found that at the very bottom layer is a deep desire to avoid abandonment. Abandonment is a very deep, dark pit.

Pastor Michael Todd speaks about the idea of the "opportunity for obscurity". He talks about the fact that God often gives us the opportunity to work through so much within the confines of obscurity. As I talked to my husband, addressing all the worries that were weighing me down, I realized how blessed I was for this opportunity to learn from this matter in private.

The thing about writing a book, sharing all of your most intimate thoughts and opinions, and even beliefs about faith, is exposing yourself to other people's criticisms and judgements. I realized that day that if I do not get this under control now, when possibly three people were upset with me, how would I handle myself when a great many more actually are offended by me, publicly disagreeing with my beliefs and theologies?

Upset stomach from worrying about the opinions and feelings of three people now, gets all gussied up in its fancy clothes, when there is a hoard of people with flaming social media pitchforks, and has the potential to turn into full-fledged hopeless thoughts of suicide. That may seem like an extreme stretch, but really, it is not. Unchecked worry turns to deep darkness when magnified. Unchecked deep darkness turns into unimaginable hopelessness. Unchecked hopelessness, well, leads down roads you sometimes cannot come back from. Again, I cannot thank God enough for the opportunity to grow through this privately, rather than in front of the masses.

I was never abandoned as a child. I have great, very human parents who did the absolute best they knew how to do. Though, I have not gotten down to the very root of the abandonment layer, I have learned I really don't have to get to that piece of the puzzle in order to operate in the freedom of acceptance and adoption by my Heavenly Father.

Romans 8:15 says,

"For you did not receive the spirit of slavery to fall back into fear, but you have received the Spirit of adoption as sons (and daughters), by whom we cry, "Abba! Father!"

I know that I am the daughter of the Most High King.

I know that I am never abandoned.

I know that I am never unwanted.

I know I am the one who Jesus loves.

I know there is a room for me in my Father's house.

These imaginary enemies who have tried to partner with me, from such a young age, have fought mercilessly to try to tell me otherwise. They have convinced me that perfect strangers did not like me.

They have persuaded me that my nearest family wanted nothing to do with me. They have convicted me of that which I was never guilty of, and always without a single shred of evidence. These imaginary enemies have been the epitome of rejection and abandonment and as tangible as they have felt at times, they just are not real. They are only imagined.

But God.

He is what is real.

He is what is tangible.

He is well proved.

"and I will be a father to you, and you shall be sons and daughters to me," says the Lord Almighty.
2 Corinthians 6:18

I believe it warrants saying again. Will you join me? Will you dare to even take a moment, right now, and close your eyes and say it with me?

I AM the child of the Most High King.

He will be a Father to me.

I am the one who Jesus loves.

Yes, I am.

Yes, you are.

Father,

I pray right now for the one reading this book, this page. I pray that the conviction that is all consuming would be lifted, that the conviction weighing heavy with lies and accusations would be removed. I pray that the yoke placed on us by imaginary enemies, would be shattered, shackles removed, and freedom embraced. Satan is so very real and not imaginary. I speak against any and all attacks he has fashioned against my family and those who are praying with You now. Please clear the cloudiness of confusion and open our eyes to see more of Your truths. Thank You for adopting us as Your own children. Thank You that abandonment is never our assignment.

I love You so!

Amen

Surely goodness and mercy shall
follow me all the days of my life,
and I shall dwell in the
house of the Lord forever.

Psalms 23:6

Only Yoked

It is always interesting to me, how various translations of scripture read the same words and verses. The postscript at the bottom of my ESV text offers that the word "surely" could be replaced with the word "only" in other translations. When I read this verse as it is written in my Bible, I see "surely" as a word of resolute certainty. I see this word as an unwavering confidence in the presence of God's goodness and mercy being ever present. I see it as being sure. But then the footnote shakes what I had built my understanding on and I get a new lens in which to view this beautiful verse.

When we replace "surely" with "only", wow! Talk about resolute certainty!

"Only goodness and mercy shall follow me all the days of my life, and I shall dwell in the house of the Lord forever."

Wow! What a confident statement that only goodness and mercy shall follow us!

One of my dear friends shared with me an incredible visual that echoes such confidence. I was sharing with her the fears and doubts I had been struggling with. That is when she shared her great wisdom with me. She said that she did not allow herself to "partner" with fear and doubt. She said that she chooses each day to partner with joy, happiness, and so much more. In that seemingly simple description, I could see my two arms linked with something else. In that moment I realized, I get to choose what I partner with. This takes me straight back to my invisible enemies.

Let us take it a step deeper. Several instances are mentioned in scripture about being yoked. It took until my adult years to understand what a yoke even was. Forgive my sheltered self. I literally thought it was an egg yolk as a child. I just had no point of reference. I literally thought the notion of being equally yoked, meant equally yolked. As a teen, I totally internalized this to mean that you had the same beliefs, which might not be too far off, but I was basing this belief on the idea of yolks being found on the inside, so our insides were the same, or equal.

For those who might have had the other oar for my childlike belief boat, let me briefly explain that a yoke is a cross bar, used to connect two animals to each other for the purpose of pulling farm equipment or transportation. This isn't about eggs. Who knew? Not the younger version of me, apparently.

If the animals are unequally yoked, neither can do their job efficiently. The weaker, or smaller, animal is under-performing, growing weaker and weaker, and the stronger, or larger, one is overcompensating and wearing out too quickly.

When we are partnered with fear and doubt, we are yoked with them. The thing about fear and doubt, they are underperformers. They are all about smoke and mirrors, illusions. They don't have any substance at all. They make you do all the work. With these ill-performing partners, you will find yourself overcompensating all of the time and wearing out easily. It is exhausting keeping up with the workload of life when you are yoked with fear and doubt.

When we are yoked with goodness and mercy, we are able to do immeasurably more than we ever thought we could. We share in the workload and accomplish so much more. Even when adversity comes, and it does, these partners keep you going. You tire much less easily, and you find you have a supernatural strength in the midst of life's demands.

Another footnote around the twenty-third Psalm notes that in place of mercy, some translations read, "steadfast love." Some of you may be like me and have a hard time internalizing the concept of mercy, but we can wrap our heads around the idea of steadfast love. It may be something foreign, never experienced by some, but nonetheless, it is something more easily grasped with our oh so human hearts.

Will you sit with that idea for a moment? The idea of goodness and steadfast love being your constant companion, can you fathom it? Our world thrives with cynicism and negativity. Our culture is quick to cancel and slow to forgive. Can you imagine what your life would look like if you could shed these unfaithful yokefellows? Can you envision a future where you surround yourself with goodness and mercy and steadfast love?

"Only goodness and mercy shall follow me all of the days of my life,"

The Psalmist had realized the value and certainty of being yoked with goodness and mercy. What great peace there is in knowing this is all you will allow to accompany you through the remainder of your days. Can you see it?

Are you willing to say goodbye to those unequal partners that have tried, with all of their might, to be yoked with you? I know they are comfortable, even in their discomfort, but are you willing to tell them it is over? They have been so faithfully unfaithful to you. They have allowed you to do all the work, and even more, just in trying to keep your head above water. They have weighed you down, pulling you down in their doubts and unbelief. They have diminished your quality of life while you have lived, sometimes barely surviving, with them at your side. Are you willing to sever ties with them once and for all, confidently stepping into partnership with the goodness and mercy God has for you, for all the days of your life?

It is a choice. It is your choice. It is my choice, too.

I know I have said it many times already, but it is true; our Good Shepherd is a gentleman. He has given you rest in green pastures. He has led you beside the still waters of reflection and nourishment. He has led and protected you in the deep darkness of the valley of the shadow of death. He saw you from a long way off, ran to you, and prepared the most incredible, redeeming feast for you. Will you take the final step and release the shackles that have bound you to the unfaithful partners you have lived your life shacked to, and step into His goodness and mercy, His steadfast love?

I know it is scary to let go of these familiar foes. But will you? What good is restoration and redemption when your choice is to stay shackled to your old self? It is as though you went from the table of redemption and right back to the trough of destitution.

The choice is all yours.

Father,
I pray for freedom. I thank You for freedom. I pray that this gift You have given us to get up and walk away, will be received. I pray that You will not let us be comfortable in the staying. That the comfortable discomfort would be no more. That we will not want to be shackled to our old self, our old ways any longer. Father, we have come so far, please do not let us go any further with old ways. We seek You true restoration and redemption.

Amen

Returning

The final verse of the twenty-third Psalm states: "*I shall dwell in the house of the Lord forever.*" At the bottom of my Bible, the word "dwell" has a special note. I love these nuggets of gold, as you have probably figured out about me. This particular little treasure states that instead of "dwell", it says "return to dwell".

I love this. No, I cherish this different look at these words.

In this book we have walked the uncomfortable journey of restoration and redemption. And now we see that the tail end of this road is not just dwelling in His house forever, it is returning to dwell. Returning is yet another choice. Don't you just love that word, choice? It is so very active on our part. He has done His part. He has gone ahead of us and prepared the way and the place for us. Now, it is our choice.

Our good Shepherd has made us to lie down in green pastures, but, for what purpose? Yes, you are right, *rest*.

We have been ushered into this opportunity for rest, reflection, redemption, and restoration. Now, in the final verse of this chapter of scripture, we see the opportunity to return to dwell with Him forever. But it is a choice.

"For thus said the Lord God, the Holy One of Israel, "In returning and rest you shall be saved; in quietness and in trust shall be your strength. But you were unwilling" Isaiah 30:15

"But you were unwilling." I want to always be found, willing, glad to return to dwell with Him forever.

Can you imagine, the Good Shepherd leading you, or trying to lead you, beside the still waters of reflection, and fighting against him? I know, it seems crazy, but, how crazy is that notion?

I do not know about you, but I find it way too easy to not do what He is calling me to do. "What's that You said Lord? I didn't hear You." "You were talking to me, Lord?" "La, la, la, la. I don't hear You." That stirring in my spirit, the quickening of my heartrate, feeling like my heart is about to beat clear out of my chest. "Push it down. Someone else will help them. He is not talking to you. Surely, He's not." "He's not calling me to make that move." "He isn't leading me to change my career path." "He would never ask me to put my heart out there, on the line, and write a book about faith. He loves me too much." Yeah, you could say I am an expert about not getting on plan with the whole letting the Shepherd lead you by still waters of reflection thing.

"But you were unwilling."

Oh, that hurts my heart. Our Heavenly Father knows, I have been so unwilling along much of my journey. I have dug my heals in and turned my heart off. And He is a gentleman, and He let me. And my life reflected how I had led myself by the stagnant waters of deflection, deflection of His calling and His purpose for my life.

But that is not the end of my story. Like you, I had a choice. I could stay in that place, or I could return to rest, to dwell in the house of the Lord.

We have talked much and often about the life of the Prodigal son. I did not have any idea that he would be so impactful to this book, but here we are again, talking about this wayward man. This young man was faced with the same choice that you and I face. He found himself at the same crossroads we are at today. He wound up in the pit of his own making, eating leftovers from pigs, because he had made such a mess of his own life, took it all into his own hands, leaving the wisdom and direction of his father. But you and I both know what he did when he literally reached the end of himself, he returned to dwell in his father's house.

Oh, the humility that surely required. Scripture even talks about he rehearsed what he would say to his father to hopefully receive undeserved grace and favor. He was prepared for rejection. He was bracing for the impact of his father disowning him. But, as we have talked about previously, his father not only accepted him back into the home, but he also gave him the family ring, embracing him into the family fold. This far-off son had a choice. I can only imagine the immeasurable relief he felt on the other side of his decision.

Another word that is used quite a bit in the New Testament is the word repent. This word is often used by legalistic, guilt tripping folks, for brow-beating people with Scriptures. But it has a powerful connection to the word we are discussing already, return. To repent is to turn away from. Sometimes, when we repent of our poor choices, our sins, we must repent and return to the positive places we came from before. One day, we will have the opportunity to repent and return to dwell with our Heavenly Father for all of eternity. I can see Him there, standing on the porch of Heaven, looking for each of us, leaping off and running to greet us, even while we are still a long way off.

Father,

Please forgive me for my straying and failing to return to You. Thank You for Your rest, Your strength, Your preparation for me. Thank You for the choice You give each of us to choose whether or not we will return to dwell with You. Father, I choose You. I choose to return to dwell with You, all of my days.

Amen

My Father's House

I remember the hot summer afternoon in Arkansas when I was just fifteen years old. My grandmother bought me an NIV Teen Study Bible. There was something different about this Bible. I could not get enough of it! I could actually read it. The style was formatted for someone my age, someone who sits in the way far back, not for the sweet little blue-haired ladies in the pews at the front of the church.

I read through it, tore through it, dog-earing pages, using gum wrappers, ripped up pieces of manilla construction paper I had found somewhere, and anything else I could get my hands on, to serve as dozens of tiny bookmarks.

I did not know that you were allowed to write in your Bible. No one had ever told me I could. I literally still have dozens upon dozens of these verses marked with torn construction paper! I found verse after verse that would help me and my friends in our times of teenage angst and struggle. I had discovered the wellspring of hope in my new Bible.

One verse offered me more hope than any other. I went to it every time I had a friend fighting the feelings of hopelessness. I deeply cherished John 14:2-4.

"In my Father's house are many rooms. If it were not so, would I have told you that I go to prepare a place for you? And if I go and prepare a place for you, I will come again and will take you to myself, that where I am you may be also. And you know the way to where I am going."

There was something hopeful about the many rooms and Him preparing a place there, for me. I felt chosen. I felt prepared for. I felt wanted for an eternity. I did not feel so abandoned.

Every time a friend would come to me with her distress, I eagerly turned to this passage of Scripture. I wanted to share with her the hope that I had found. I wanted to show her that we have a place for all of eternity. I wanted to show her that she too, is chosen, prepared for, and wanted, even if, no especially if, her troubling issue was a hairy legged boy giving her a hard time.

Friend, I want you to know the same. Oh, that I wish I could come to your home, sit with you on your front porch, pull out my teen study Bible, turn to the Winterfresh™ wrapper in John 14 and pour my hopeful guts out to you. I wish that I could sit with you in whatever it is that is trying to hold onto you, trying desperately to continue to yoke itself with you, and give you hope that partnering with goodness and mercy is so good. Oh, that I could read to you about the many rooms, and Jesus preparing the way before us.

Do you think that the banquet table spoken of in the twenty-third Psalm is in this house? What about the captive guests? Is it possible that the still water lingers through the green pastures around the house? What if this is the house of the Lord that we are to dwell in forever? Maybe all of this is the hope that draws me near. Maybe all of this is why I long to share all of it with you.

Will you sit with me a little longer? Let us sit together on the front porch of our hearts, and talk about the house, the rooms, the preparation, the adoption, the redemption. I will fix some sweet tea. Will you stay a little longer?

Father,
Thank You for this place in Scripture that has drawn my heart to Yours since the first time I laid eyes on it. Thank You for preparing a place for me to dwell all of my days and all of my forever. Thank You for the visual of seeing this all come together in You. Thank You for being in the details of life. I love You, so!

Amen

Length of Days

When reading this final verse of the twenty-third Psalm, I see another footnote at the bottom of my Bible that explains the word "forever" is read as "length of days" in the Hebrew context.

I do not know about you, but forever can seem like an unfathomable length of time. It almost does not seem real because it was before us and will continue after us. We cannot measure it. We cannot touch it. It just seems so ambiguous to me. But when I read "length of days" something seemed accessible, relatable, to me. I get that it means the same thing as forever, but somehow the words "length of days" seems to jump off the page of my red lined Bible and commit to walk alongside me as I go through this day-to-day life.

In the cool air of Fall, hangs the red-hot heat from the election cycle. Tensions are high and morale's are low. The jabs have been flying across the bow for many months, well sadly, years now. The country we live in has become so polarized, many from even the same families, refusing to come to the table of common ground.

Each of us personally know only a handful of people who would be with us through thick and thin. But who could we say would be with us the length of days? Our parents who were with us since our conception? No, sadly many of them will pass before we do. Who then? Our mate? No, though they have been around a long time, they were not with us from the beginning. Noone found on this Earth will be with us the length of our days, besides our Heavenly Father.

King David knew this. He found solace in this.

He penned the words that jumped off the pages of a red-lined Bible, because they were his real experience. He walked hand in hand with the one who was with him the length of days. And he wrote it down for himself, for others to find hope in, for you, for me. That we too, would find solace in knowing that we would, we could, spend the length of our days, dwelling in the house of the Lord, too.

Your invitation is written in the scriptures, delivered in the death and resurrection of Christ, and now, it is in your hands. Will you accept the invitation? Will you return to dwell in His house for the length of days, with the great Shepherd? It is your choice to make.

Thank You, Father, that we get to dwell with you forever, for the length of days! Thank you for going and preparing a place for you, a place that you planned well in advance for us! Thank you for loving us enough to come and take us with you. I love you so!

Amen

Just Tell Them That I Did It

Some time ago, I saw the sweetest movie. A tender, heart-wrenching Christian film. Like all great Christian movies, I left feeling like I could do anything, conquer anything, for and in Christ.

In my quiet thoughts, on our way home, I found myself thinking about my little side business. I remembered a dear, wise friend who said she used her not so little makeup side gig to do women's ministry with every woman she got to work with. How cool! Every tube of lipstick sold, was an opportunity to do life with another woman, face to face, heart to heart. She was called to share the foundation of the gospel and how He cleansed her life through the sharing of her testimony, all over cosmetic foundations and facial cleansers.

I told God all about how I wanted my business to glorify Him, and it be a way for me to do His work, just like this inspiring woman. But, in my inner thoughts I told Him, I did not want to use Him to get business. And I kid you not, I heard a quiet voice say, "You tell them that I did it."

"When the glories of life come, just tell them I did it. When victory comes. When redemption comes. Just tell them that I did it."

Ok Lord. I will.

Please do not read that wrong. Never did He say that I should take the glory for what has been done. He is saying to tell them that He did it, not me. "Just tell them that I did it." He is the "I" in all of that. His call to action is for me to tell the world, the one person, anyone who will listen, that He did it.

How often have I gotten tongue tied when trying to share my faith with others? How many times have I gotten lost in my own head, worrying about what I should or should not say? I have always wanted to give Him the glory but did not know how overcomplicated I was making it.

"Just tell them that I did it."

This morning, I found myself reading the Scripture again, of the Samaritan woman at the well. As we discussed before, the verses in John say that Jesus basically reads her diary right back to her, well not literally. He reveals Himself and the totality of who He is, by intimately knowing all about her innermost private details. He shares knowledge of her that no stranger should have been privy to, and most who knew her well probably also did not know. He did not regurgitate gossip. He poured out intimate knowledge of her. This blew her away. Her response? She went to town to go tell everyone,

"He told me all that I ever did." John 4:39

And the scriptures go on to say that many believed in Him because of her words.

Did you catch her not so complicated testimony? Eight words. *"He told me all that I ever did."* His intimate knowledge of her was all that she needed to know that

He was the promised Messiah. And all Scripture tells us that her testimony was held within eight little, simple, understated words. She did not have a PowerPoint, or a deep, meaning-filled song, or a long drawn out, gut wrenching story of a life lived before Christ and a life lived after. She simply did exactly what He was calling me to do. She told them any and all who would listen that He did it.

If you have made the choice to leave the shackles of your old yokes behind and chosen to be yoked with Jesus, the one who died and rose for your eternal freedom, you have the call to share what He has done in your life.

This is where I have gotten it all wrong and all jumbled up. This is where I have overcomplicated something so simple and beautiful. The gift of salvation He has given me, is the story of hope He has given me, to in turn give away to others. He did it. I did not. I was lost in my wanderings and He found me. I did not find myself. He was looking for me. He ran to greet me when I was still covered in trough leftovers. I tried to fix me with every book study known to man. They put bandages on my bleeding soul, but each bandage quickly became blood drenched and needing replacement.

I needed something more than I could give myself. I needed a Savior. I am not my own savior. I am fully human. I was fully broken. He is fully whole. He did it. He died. He rose. He offered me this gift. I pretended to receive. I walked around still fully broken with various Christian masks on. He offered me this gift, time and time again. I went through the motions of praying the prayers. I tried to earn the gift He was giving freely. I tried time and time again, in vain, to pay Him back for this precious gift. I never could repay, or earn, or be good or whole enough to receive the gift. Then I learned my role was to receive.

No more blood drenched bandages. No more self-driven fixes. No more standing in line, endlessly, trying to pay for this gift. No more Christian masks.
I just earnestly received the gift and tell them He did it. Simple.

My testimony tripped me up for years.

"What do I tell them?"

"What do I say?"

"My life wasn't as bad as so many other people."

"They won't get anything from what I have to say."

"Just tell them that I did it."

And I have.

I have told them of the life He has redeemed. I have told of the marriage that He has resurrected. I have told them of the children who have turned out well beyond our hopes, dreams, and prayers, despite our terrible parenting, because His grace covered each of them. I have told them that He did it.

The ability to walk, no run, even for short, thuddy distances, He did it. The ability to conquer the foods that kept me in shackles for decades, He did it. The words written to you today, the courage to even write them at all, He did it. And He gets any glory that comes from any of this life I have lived.

"But for me it is good to be near God; I have made the Lord God my refuge, that I may tell of all your works."
Psalm 73:28

"that they may see and know, may consider and understand together, that the hand of the Lord has done this, the Holy One of Israel has created it."
Isaiah 41:20

Father,

Thank You for redemption. Thank You for being the one who rights the wrongs. Thank You for showing us that it is not that complicated. Thank You for showing us that we can give You glory in simply pointing them all back to You. Let us not mistake Your hand at work in our lives, believing that it was ours. Your Word says that You are our strength and our song. I praise You all of my days! Thank You for writing Your word on my heart and allowing me to share it with the world around me, knees shaking, heart open for all to see. May Your word not return to You void. May each reader, see Your light, Your hope, Your restoration, and Your redemption. May we all come running home to You, our good and perfect Shepherd. May we live to tell of Your mighty works in our lives, telling them all that You did it! I love You, so!

Bryn